WHAT YOU DON'T KNOW CAN HURT YOU

WHAT YOU DON'T KNOW CAN HURT YOU:

Destroying the Deception Surrounding Prosperity

by
RayGene Wilson

Harrison House, Inc.
Tulsa, Oklahoma

What You Don't Know Can Hurt You:
Destroying the Deception Surrounding Prosperity
ISBN 1-57794-211-6
Copyright © 1999 by RayGene Wilson
P.O. Box 4779
Tulsa, Oklahoma 74159

Published by Harrison House, Inc.
P.O. Box 35035
Tulsa, Oklahoma 74153

CONTENTS

FOREWORD BY JESSE DUPLANTIS

What a refreshing book! Straightforward, doctrinally sound and full of insight from God's Word, RayGene has taken a very misunderstood subject and created an easy reading book that I believe will completely change the way you view abundance. I so enjoyed my time reading this book that I had to stop and do a little shouting! Kick the devil around a little bit, just for fun! I could preach many sermons from just one chapter—and, glory to God, I believe I will! It's *that* good!

You see, nothing excites me more than the truth of God's Word. And this book is most certainly filled with that. This isn't just RayGene's opinion. It's what the Word says about prosperity. Forget the traditional religious rhetoric. RayGene cuts through all of that and gets to the heart of this issue. You'll find out how to sow your seed the "right" way and discover the importance of watching what you say. You'll learn what you've been redeemed from, what Jesus had to say about prosperity and, most importantly, what you can start expecting to receive. By the end of this book, you won't have a shadow of doubt about what's true and what's not. You'll *know* the myths from the truth. And that truth *will* set you free! Glory!

So, come on! Grab a cup of coffee or a glass of iced tea, find a spot to curl up in and get ready to be blessed. But before you do, let me warn you about something: God's Word is alive. When you get a revelation of God's will for your prosperity, you just might find yourself standing up and declaring, "Hey, devil! Now that I know what's true, hurtin' is comin' your way!"

—*Jesse Duplantis*

PREFACE

This book is designed to paint a picture of God's plan for the prosperity of His Church in the last days. If you know someone who is confused about the prosperity message, or if you yourself aren't sure about it, then this is the book for you. In it I endeavor to show you what the Bible says about prosperity and what God has revealed to me about it from my own study of the Scriptures.

However, it's important for you to read the book with an open mind and a teachable spirit. Don't just take my word for everything. Study the Scriptures we cover for yourself with the guidance of the Holy Spirit. Remember, God is not out to get you. He is out to help you. But He can't help you if you won't let Him.

You have to read and study the Word of God for yourself and appropriate what it says into your own life. You must get as much knowledge as you can so that you can then act in faith on what you know. God's Word says His people are destroyed from lack of knowledge. (Hos. 4:6.) In other words, *what you don't know can hurt you.*

WHAT YOU MUST KNOW

Prosperity is not just having money. True prosperity is wholeness in every area.

Of course, it's most important to be prosperous spiritually because the Bible says your financial and physical prosperity are contingent on the prosperity of your soul.

Beloved, I wish above all things that thou mayest prosper and be in health, even as thy soul prospereth.

3 John 2

You may hear many different theories on biblical prosperity, but the Bible is clear about how God wants to provide for you. The dozens of Scriptures we will cover in this book—from both the Old and the New Testaments—have the same thread of truth running through them. By the time you have finished reading, you will see the true nature of your Father God and His desire to bless and prosper His children.

It's important to study carefully what the Bible says about prosperity, because it is not just *the truth* that sets you free; it's *the truth that you know* that sets you free.

There are some principles you just have to know before you can see the blessings of God's abundance manifesting in your life. It's my purpose in this book to tell you what these principles are so that you will know the truth of God's abundance and will be able to walk in greater prosperity in all areas of your life.

chapter one

REDEEMED FROM POVERTY

As believers, we talk much about our redemption from spiritual death[1] through the blood of Jesus—and we should. But what we often don't realize is that when we were redeemed from spiritual death, something else was also happening in that redemption. The same precious blood that was shed to redeem us from spiritual death was also shed *at the same time* to redeem us from the threefold curse of the law.

Now, make no mistake about it, redemption from spiritual death is the most important thing. The most important thing is that you make heaven and miss hell. But if going to heaven when you die is all you get out of your redemption, you are falling short of what Jesus paid for.

One-third of your redemption has to do with what happens when you leave earth and move to heaven. But two-thirds of your redemption has to do with what is going on while you are still here: your redemption from poverty and your redemption from sickness.

THE CURSE OF THE LAW

In his letter to the Galatians, the apostle Paul reminds us that as Christians we have been redeemed from something he calls the "curse of the law."

Christ hath redeemed us from the curse of the law, being made a curse for us: for it is written, Cursed is every one that hangeth on a tree: That the blessing of Abraham might come on the Gentiles through Jesus Christ; that we might receive the promise of the Spirit through faith.

And if ye be Christ's, then are ye Abraham's seed, and heirs according to the promise.

Galatians 3:13,14,29

That sounds wonderful, doesn't it? But what, exactly, does it mean? You need to know, because if you are redeemed from something but don't know what it is, your redemption won't do you any good.

Just what *is* the "curse of the law"? To find out, we have to go back to the Law—the first five books of the Old Testament. In these books, we find that the penalty for breaking God's law is threefold: spiritual death, poverty and sickness. And the reward for keeping God's law is also threefold: life, prosperity and health. The penalties are called *curses,* and the rewards are called *blessings.*

BLESSINGS AND CURSES

Chapter 28 of Deuteronomy gives an account of the blessings and curses. This account is so plain and easy to understand, it is surprising that so many Christians are confused by it. I am going to point out the blessings first, and then we will go over the curses. The blessings are described in the first fourteen verses.

And it shall come to pass, if thou shalt hearken diligently unto the voice of the Lord thy God, to observe and to do all his commandments which I command thee this day, that the Lord thy God will set thee on high above all nations of the earth: And all these blessings shall come on thee, and overtake thee, if thou shalt hearken unto the voice of the Lord thy God. Blessed shalt thou be in the city, and blessed shalt thou be in the field. Blessed shall be the fruit of thy body, and the fruit of thy ground, and the fruit of thy cattle, the increase of thy kine, and the flocks of thy sheep. Blessed shall be thy basket and thy store. Blessed shalt thou be when thou comest in, and blessed shalt thou be when thou goest out. The Lord shall cause thine enemies that rise up against thee to be smitten before thy face: they shall come out against thee one way, and flee before thee seven ways. The Lord shall command the blessing upon thee in thy storehouses, and in all that thou settest thine hand unto; and he shall bless thee in the land which the Lord thy God giveth thee. The Lord shall establish thee an holy people unto himself, as he hath sworn unto thee, if thou shalt keep the commandments of the Lord thy God, and walk in his ways. And all people of the earth shall see that thou art called by the name of the Lord; and they shall be afraid of thee. And the Lord shall make thee plenteous in goods, in the fruit of thy body, and in the fruit of thy cattle, and in the fruit of thy ground, in the land which the Lord sware unto thy fathers to give thee. The Lord shall open unto thee his good treasure, the heaven to give the rain unto thy

land in his season, and to bless all the work of thine hand: and thou shalt lend unto many nations, and thou shalt not borrow. And the Lord shall make thee the head, and not the tail; and thou shalt be above only, and thou shalt not be beneath; if that thou hearken unto the commandments of the Lord thy God, which I command thee this day, to observe and to do them: And thou shalt not go aside from any of the words which I command thee this day, to the right hand, or to the left, to go after other gods to serve them.

Deuteronomy 28:1-14

It is easy to see from these verses that blessings from God are not only spiritual. They are also material. Blessings on cattle and sheep and on baskets and storehouses don't have to do with your spiritual life. They have to do with your natural life. Of course, increase of flocks and herds and harvests of grain may not be very meaningful to modern city dwellers, but farmers know what these verses mean. If you're not a farmer, just translate these blessings into financial terms. For instance, verse 8 speaks about our storehouses. Most of us have one, but we are likely to call it a bank account or a savings plan today.

However, the point I'm making is that these Scriptures prove that being prosperous is not ungodly. On the contrary, prosperity was God's idea in the first place. According to the Bible, all these blessings should literally be running after us and overtaking us. All we have to do to be blessed is to stop running away from them and let them catch up.

MISQUOTES AND MISCONCEPTIONS

Why do we so often run away from the prosperity God wants us to have? Usually it's because we have heard so much about poverty in connection with God that some people have gotten the mistaken idea that it is godly to be poor. People have even taken vows of poverty and been praised for it.

Now, don't get me wrong. I don't doubt these are well-meaning people, but living in poverty does not line up with the Bible. You don't find God ever being poor or telling us we are supposed to be in poverty. That teaching comes from religion and from people who take Scriptures out of context to back up their mistaken beliefs. Certain Scriptures are often misquoted and misused to back up these misconceptions about biblical prosperity.

CAN A RICH MAN SERVE GOD?

One of these misunderstood passages comes from Luke 16:13.

No servant can serve two masters: for either he will hate the one, and love the other; or else he will hold to the one, and despise the other. Ye cannot serve God and mammon.

In the context of what Jesus was saying, that last statement is absolutely true. You can't serve God—put Him in first place in your life—and serve mammon, that is, continue to put money in first place in your life. But Jesus wasn't saying you can't serve God if you have money. He was saying you have to put money in its proper place. Money is nothing more than a tool. And Jesus was telling His disciples they should *serve* God but *use* money.

This verse is often misused to prove that a person who has money cannot serve God. But that's nonsense. Of course a rich man can serve God. A rich man can serve God just as well as a poor man can. In fact, having money may make it easier for a man to serve God. Service to God has nothing to do with a person's money. Service to God has to do with a person's heart.

CAN A RICH MAN ENTER HEAVEN?

Another mistaken idea about God's attitude toward money is that a rich person can't go to heaven. This myth seems to come from a misreading of what Jesus said about the camel and the eye of the needle.

Then said Jesus unto his disciples, Verily I say unto you, That a rich man shall hardly enter into the kingdom of heaven. And again I say unto you, It is easier for a camel to go through the eye of a needle, than for a rich man to enter into the kingdom of God.

Matthew 19:23,24

What is Jesus really talking about here? Is He really saying that a person who has money will be excluded from heaven when he dies?

Again we have to say, "Of course not." The problem comes from people who confuse the phrase "kingdom of God" with "heaven." The phrase "kingdom of God" does not refer only to heaven. A better definition of the kingdom of God is [God's] **way of doing** [things] **and being right** (Matt. 6:33 AMP). Or we could say that the kingdom of God is God's *system,* His way of doing things or His "lifestyle" here on earth.

Since Jesus said that His disciples should **seek...first the kingdom of God, and his righteousness** (Matt. 6:33) and **where your treasure is, there will your heart be also** (Matt. 6:21), it would be hard for a rich man to enter into God's kingdom if his heart were in his riches. Therefore, a better way to read Matthew 19:23 might be as follows: "It is hard for a rich man to enter into God's way of doing things if he is trusting in his money instead of in God." In fact, that's what Jesus did say in Mark's version of the story.

And Jesus looked round about, and saith unto his disciples, How hardly shall they that have riches enter into the kingdom of God! And the disciples were astonished at his words. But Jesus answereth again, and saith unto them, Children, how hard is it for them that *trust in riches* to enter into the kingdom of God.

Mark 10:23,24

So we see that Jesus was not telling rich people they couldn't go to heaven. He was saying it would be hard for them to enter into God's way of doing things here on earth if they trusted in their money instead of in God.

IS MONEY THE ROOT OF ALL EVIL?

First Timothy 6:10 is one of the most misquoted verses in the Bible. It is usually quoted as "Money is the root of all evil." But that's not what Paul said. He said, **The love of money is the root of all evil.** Money itself is not the root of all evil; it's the *love of money* that is the root of all evil. In other words, the root of all evil is the desire for money, or greed.

Now, this is an interesting Scripture. We usually apply it to people who have a lot of money, but let me tell you, there are people committing that sin who don't have a dime. In fact, it's been my experience that the less money you have, the more you are likely to love it.

At the times in my life when my wife and I were broke and in debt, if someone gave me a $100 bill, I cherished it. Of course, I didn't *say* that I loved it, because I know the Bible tells me I should not love money. But I have to admit that I treated that $100 dollars as if I loved it. Why? Because I didn't see many $100 bills in those days. In the world, anything that is relatively scarce or hard to come by, like gold or diamonds, is precious. Likewise, when I didn't have much, any money I did get was precious to me.

Now, of course, I view a $100 bill as merely a tool. A tool for what? For building the kingdom of God. Now I see money as a tool to help in bringing in the end-time harvest of souls, the precious fruit of the entire earth.

YOU DON'T HAVE TO STAY BROKE

I recently heard someone say, "You can go to heaven broke, but because you go to heaven broke, someone else may not get to go." That is why **the wealth of the sinner is laid up for the just** (Prov. 13:22). Wealth is for the Church to bring in the harvest in the last days. And it is going to take a lot of money to do it. You can be on the outside looking in if you want to, but I'm determined to be right in the middle of what God is doing.

However, if you are broke, you don't have to stay that way. The Bible calls being broke a curse, and we've just learned that God doesn't want us to live under a curse.

THE CURSES

As we've just seen, the first part of Deuteronomy 28 tells us what we have been redeemed *to*—the blessings. The rest of the chapter tells us in great detail what we have been redeemed *from*—the curses.

But it shall come to pass, if thou wilt not hearken unto the voice of the Lord thy God, to observe to do all his commandments and his statutes which I command thee this day; that all these curses shall come upon thee, and overtake thee: Cursed shalt thou be in the city, and cursed shalt thou be in the field. Cursed shall be thy basket and thy store. Cursed shall be the fruit of thy body, and the fruit of thy land, the increase of thy kine, and the flocks of thy sheep. Cursed shalt thou be when thou comest in, and cursed shalt thou be when thou goest out.

And...*thou shalt not prosper in thy ways:* and thou shalt be only oppressed and spoiled evermore, and no man shall save thee.

Deuteronomy 28:15-19,29

And so it goes on for fifty-four verses—almost three times as many curses as there are blessings. All these terrible calamities should befall all of us because we were all sinners. But thank God, Christ has **redeemed us from the curse of the law, being made a curse for us** (Gal. 3:13). Poverty is a curse and does not belong to you if you are a child of God.

THE SAME STANDARD

Sometimes we act as if God's standard of judging what is good for us and what is bad for us is different than our standards. However, that's not true. *Good* means the same thing to God as it does to you.

The Bible says in Acts 10:38 that Jesus **went about doing good, and healing all that were oppressed of the devil.** We can easily see from this Scripture that healing is good because it comes from God, and sickness is oppression from the devil.

Obviously, the Bible says healing is good and sickness is bad. I'm sure most people would agree. Why then do some of these same people say that a certain person is in the hospital because God is trying to teach him or her something? Sometimes you even hear people say that God gave them the sickness or disease or caused the accident. How many of you would break your little child's arm or make him sick just to teach him something? I hope none of you. Only abusive parents do things to harm their children. Why would we think God could be so cruel?

As a matter of fact, Jesus asked the same question.

> **Or what man is there of you, whom if his son ask bread, will he give him a stone? Or if he ask a fish, will he give him a serpent? If ye then, being evil, know how to give good gifts unto your children, how much more shall your Father which is in heaven give good things to them that ask him?**
>
> **Matthew 7:9-11**

Here Jesus says plainly that God gives *good* things to His children. It is difficult to see how anyone can misinterpret what the Lord is saying, but many times they do. The people who think God gave them an illness don't seem to realize how illogical their thinking is. If you truly thought the sickness was from God in the first place, why would you even go to the hospital to try to get rid of something God gave you? If you truly thought it was God's will for you to be sick, why would you spend money on medicine to try to get out of the will of God? Why not just really glorify Him and suffer as much as you can with it?

The answer is that you don't really believe it in your heart yourself. Someone just said it, and it sounded nice and religious, so you repeated it.

PROSPERITY IS GOOD

In the area of prosperity, people also get the idea that God has a different system of values than ours. But once again, *good* means the same thing to God as it does to us. I can prove that by the Bible. For instance, God not only told Adam where gold could be found in the Garden of Eden, but He also told Adam that gold is good.

And a river went out of Eden to water the garden; and from thence it was parted, and became into four heads. The name of the first is Pison: that is it which compasseth the whole land of Havilah, *where there is gold; And the gold of that land is good....*

Genesis 2:10-12

Man wouldn't have known gold from dirt if God hadn't told him. But God told him where the gold was and said it was good. If you have any gold, you already know it is good.

The Bible says prosperity is good and poverty is bad. If you have ever been in poverty, you know how horrible it is. It is ungodly not to be able to buy clothes for your children to wear or food for them to eat. In traveling around the world, Beth and I have seen poverty everywhere, but you don't have to go far to find it. It is in your town—maybe right next door.

Usually, you find the most ungodly activity in the most poverty-stricken areas. Crime, drug abuse and disease run rampant in those areas.

Many religious people who take a vow of poverty and go to live in an organized religious community like a monastery or convent are not living in poverty at all. Often they are living in mansions. Many times when we minister in Europe, Beth and I stay in places like this instead of in hotels. These are some of the most elaborate places you can imagine. The floors are marble, there is plenty of food and all their clothes are provided. That doesn't sound too bad to me.

That is not real poverty. Real poverty is the homeless person huddled in a doorway with rags tied around him, begging for food so he can have something to eat today. That is poverty, and there is nothing good or godly about it.

FINDING THE SOURCE

There's an easy way to find out if something is from God or the devil. We can use the Bible to distinguish between the two. The Word of God gives us very plain guidelines to follow in determining the origin of things. Let's look at what Jesus said.

> **The thief cometh not, but for to steal, and to kill, and to destroy: I am come that they might have life, and that they might have it more abundantly.**
>
> **John 10:10**

I like the way *The Amplified Bible* expands the meaning of this verse.

> **The thief comes only in order to steal and kill and destroy. I came that they may have and enjoy life, and have it in abundance (to the full, till it overflows).**

By this we know that if something has to do with stealing anything from you, killing, or taking of life, or destruction, then the author is the devil. If it has to do with an abundant, prosperous, healthy life, lived to the maximum capacity, it came from God.

A PRAYER FOR PROSPERITY

In his letter to his friend and disciple Gaius, the apostle John prays that his friend will enjoy health and prosperity.

> **Beloved, I wish above all things that thou mayest prosper and be in health, even as thy soul prospereth.**
>
> **3 John 2**

The word "wish" in the *King James Version* is not a good translation from the original text. A better word here would be "pray."[2] As a matter of fact, *The Amplified Bible* and most other modern translations, such as the *New International Version* and *The Living Bible,* use the word "pray" instead of "wish" in this verse.

Now, this is a very interesting verse because it is difficult to distort the meaning here, even for an anti-prosperity preacher. You will never see those people use this verse, because when they see the word "rich" or "prosperous" in the Bible, they immediately say "that is only spiritually speaking" without even seeing the meaning of the whole text. Anyone who is preaching against biblical prosperity can't use this verse, because it talks about the prosperity of the soul *and* natural prosperity. No one can say John is speaking only spiritually here, because he specifically mentions natural prosperity and health. As a matter of fact, the natural prosperity and health listed here are contingent on the prosperity of your soul.

A PROSPEROUS SOUL

Spiritual prosperity[3] should be everyone's number-one priority. The worst thing that can happen to you is to be prosperous materially without prospering in your soul. If you have a lot of financial prosperity but are living a carnal life in the world, prosperity will only help you live a more ungodly life. In this case, your prosperity only gives you more money to consume on your lusts, whatever they happen to be.

People who see a wealthy person living in sin say, "See, that's what money will do for you." However, the problem really has nothing to do with money, but with the fool who has the money.

That is why natural prosperity is contingent on the prosperity of your soul, that is, on the prosperity of your inner man. I have heard people say, "So-and-so got a lot of money, and he quit going to church. He got a boat and started going to the lake on Sundays." What these people are trying to prove is that that is what happens when a Christian gets money.

But the failure to be faithful in going to church has nothing to do with the money. It has to do with the inner character of the person who has the money. The money just revealed the character which was already there on the inside of that person.

Having more money will also give you more opportunity to do more for the kingdom of God. God isn't looking at whether you have money or not. He looks at the state of your inner man.

The Lord seeth not as man seeth; for man looketh on the outward appearance, but the Lord looketh on the heart.

1 Samuel 16:7

THE RIGHT EMPHASIS

We know prosperity is a good thing, because the apostle John prays that we would have it above all else. This prayer is just as much for us today as it was when John first wrote it. The Bible is God speaking to each of us. You can easily see now why the apostle was praying for health and prosperity. He must have looked 2000 years down the road and seen the attacks that would come on believers in the areas of prosperity and healing. When you start talking about those two subjects, you can wake up more persecutors than you can stir with a stick. And that's just the Christians. With brothers and sisters like that, who needs the devil?

We said at the beginning of this chapter that redemption from spiritual death is only one-third of what Jesus purchased for us by His blood shed on the cross. But if we have been redeemed from the *threefold* curse of the law, why do we treat the parts of our threefold redemption so differently? Why do we put different emphasis and importance on some things but act as if others aren't even there?

If Jesus shed His blood to redeem us from spiritual death, poverty and sickness, why do we act as if He only did one-third of His job? We are convinced that He redeemed us from hell. No one could talk us out of that. But we are often led astray by demonic teachings that say sickness and poverty are of God.

PUT EQUAL VALUE ON ALL PARTS
OF YOUR REDEMPTION

Now, follow me with this for a moment. What if someone went on Christian television and said there were no such thing as heaven or salvation? If someone did that on Christian television, most of you would make phone calls to the station—and you should. You would write letters to the station managers—and you should. Someone would probably organize a petition in the vestibule of the church to sign up names in protest. You might even staple a huge poster to a stick and go march in circles around their building.

But what if someone on Christian television said that God gave them a sickness to teach them something? You might not like it; you might turn off the television in disgust, but I doubt you would make any phone calls. Why? That unscriptural statement doesn't bother you as much as the other one does. And yet the precious blood of Jesus paid for your redemption from sickness at the same time that it paid for your redemption from spiritual death.

Okay, now, what if someone got on Christian television and said God didn't want to bless you with prosperity? Most of the time, that doesn't even bother us at all. As a matter of fact, you can write a book on how God doesn't want to bless His people financially, and the book will show up on the Christian bestseller list. And yet the blood of Jesus paid for prosperity at the same time that it paid for eternal life. If you really think about it, when you talk against the blessings of God, you are talking against the blood of Jesus.

Now, I am not trying to get anyone to go out and organize a protest. I am just trying to prove a point about how we put different values on different parts of our redemption, while God values them all the same. He puts equal value on all of our redemption. One-third of our redemption has to do with when we leave here, but until that time comes, *God's will and plan for us is to live healthy, prosperous lives.* The Bible is not written for heaven. You won't need it there. The Bible is written for us to use here and now.

When you truly get the revelation that you have been redeemed from the threefold curse of the law, it will change your whole Christian life. Your walk with God will take on a whole new light because you will begin to see Him in a new way. Oral Roberts was greatly persecuted years ago when he coined the phrase "God is a good God." Can you imagine Christians getting mad at you for saying that?

God *is* a good God. And He only has good things to give you. If anything good happens to you, God is the author of it. Thank God we have not only been redeemed from spiritual death, but from sickness and from poverty. And this **so great**

salvation (Heb. 2:3), this great redemption from the threefold curse of the law, is all because of the precious blood of Jesus.

chapter two

GOD IS NOT BALANCED

"Balance" is a word which I believe has robbed us more than any other. We hear a great deal about "balance," but often what people really mean by being "balanced" is just being "average." Don't be "extreme." Don't be "extravagant." Stay in the middle of the road, and don't have too much of anything.

But the interesting thing to me is that *God is not balanced at all.* Everything He does is overdone. *Extreme* and *extravagant* are words that describe God. You have never seen "over the top" until you've seen how God does things.

We usually bring up the concept of balance when we are talking about prosperity. We don't think about balance when it comes to any other part of our redemption. Why do we only think of being balanced, or average, on the prosperity part? To find out, let's take another look at all of our redemption and see why we differentiate among spiritual death, healing and prosperity.

SPIRITUAL DEATH

Spiritual death does not belong to any of us. We have been redeemed from it by the blood of Jesus.

For God so loved the world, that he gave his only begotten Son, that whosoever believeth in him should not perish, but have everlasting life. For God sent not his Son into the world to condemn the world; but that the world through him might be saved.

John 3:16,17

Jesus died to save the whole world, but the whole world is not saved. Why not? Because the whole world has not yet believed in Jesus as Lord and received that salvation. Just because Jesus purchased your redemption does not mean you automatically have it or are enjoying the benefits of it. Redemption won't do you any good if you don't receive it.

Everything that belongs to you as a child of God, you have to obtain by faith. The entire kingdom of God operates on this principle. If you think about it, you will realize there are people who die and go to hell every day. And yet Jesus redeemed them from hell by His precious blood. No one has to go to hell. In fact, no one should go to hell.

God is not balanced about your redemption from hell and spiritual death. As far as God is concerned, redemption belongs to everyone all the time. Whether you receive it or not is up to you, but God is completely one-sided about it. He is absolutely extreme about it. Jesus paid the price for everyone. He does not show partiality to anyone. As the Bible says in Romans 2:11, **There is no respect of persons with God.**

SICKNESS AND DISEASE

If you are saved, you have been redeemed from sickness and disease. Jesus took them for you, and healing belongs to everyone. What He bore on the cross, you need not bear.

But he was wounded for our transgressions, he was bruised for our iniquities: the chastisement of our peace was upon him; and with his stripes we are healed.

Isaiah 53:5

Who his own self bare our sins in his own body on the tree, that we, being dead to sins, should live unto righteousness: by whose stripes ye were healed.

1 Peter 2:24

It is easy to see from these Scriptures that healing belongs to everyone. No one is left out. God is totally one-sided about healing. He is absolutely extreme about it. The entire emphasis of Jesus' ministry when He walked on the earth was teaching, preaching and healing. He went about healing everywhere He went. The Bible says **He went about doing good, and healing all who were oppressed of the devil** (Acts 10:38).

However, as we said in the case of redemption from spiritual death, just because Jesus paid the price for you to be healed, that does not mean you are automatically healed. You have to do something to receive healing, just as you do with everything else that belongs to you as a child of God. You have to receive it by faith. However, as far as God is concerned, it already belongs to everyone.

31

POVERTY

Second Corinthians 8:9 is probably one of the most debated Scriptures in the Bible. It says,

For ye know the grace of our Lord Jesus Christ, that, though he was rich, yet for your sakes he became poor, that ye through his poverty might be rich.

The most common misreading of this verse is that Paul is speaking of *spiritual* riches, not *natural* riches. However, there are two easy ways to find out if that interpretation is correct.

The first way is to ask, "What is the context or the subject in this whole passage of Scripture?" The subjects of chapters 8 and 9 of 2 Corinthians are giving and money. Paul is writing to the Corinthian believers about their part in an offering of money that is being collected for the relief of a famine in Jerusalem. He wants to be sure they have their offering ready when his messengers come to pick it up. The first three verses of chapter 9 make this clear.

I realize that I really don't even need to mention this to you, about helping God's people. For I know how eager you are to do it, and I have boasted to the friends in Macedonia that you were ready to send an offering a year ago. In fact, it was this enthusiasm of yours that stirred up many of them to begin helping. But I am sending these men just to be sure that you really are ready, as I told them you would be, with your money all collected; I don't want it to turn out that this time I was wrong in my boasting about you.

2 Corinthians 9:1-3 TLB

From these verses we can see plainly that this entire section of Paul's letter is about money. Therefore, to pull one verse out and say it is talking about something else is completely inconsistent with the rest of the text.

The second way we can determine whether 2 Corinthians 8:9 is speaking of spiritual or natural riches is to ask, "Did Jesus become poor spiritually, if that is what it means?" The verse says **yet for your sakes he became *poor.*** I don't think anyone could truthfully say Jesus was poor spiritually. How many spiritually poor people do you see walking around without sin, raising the dead, healing the sick and the paralyzed and setting people free from all kinds of bondage?

The answer is none!

Of course Jesus didn't become poor spiritually. One way He became poor was in leaving the wealth of heaven.

HEAVEN'S WEALTH

Have you ever read what the Bible says heaven is like?

The city was laid out like a square, as long as it was wide. He measured the city with the rod and found it to be 12,000 stadia [about 1,500 miles] **in length, and as wide and high as it is long. He measured its wall and it was 144 cubits** [about 72 yards] **thick, by man's measurement, which the angel was using. The wall was made of jasper, and the city of pure gold, as pure as glass. The foundations of the city walls were decorated with every kind of precious stone. The first foundation was jasper, the second sapphire, the third chalcedony, the fourth emerald, the fifth sardonyx, the sixth carnelian, the seventh chrysolite, the eighth beryl, the ninth topaz, the tenth chrysoprase, the eleventh jacinth, and the twelfth amethyst. The twelve gates were twelve pearls, each**

**gate made of a single pearl. The great street of the city
was of pure gold, like transparent glass.**

Revelation 21:16-21 NIV

We often say heaven has streets paved with gold. But that
isn't the way the Bible describes them. To say that streets are
paved with gold would mean they are *gold plated*. But the
streets of heaven are not gold plated. There is not just a layer of
gold on top. The streets of heaven *are* gold all the way through.

And not only are heaven's streets made of gold, but the entire
city, which is 1,500 miles long, 1,500 miles wide and 1,500 miles
high, is solid gold. There is no place on earth with that kind of
wealth. Now, if you left that behind and came to the earth, even
to the best and most beautiful place on earth, you can easily see
how you would become poor. The dusty roads of Palestine Jesus
walked on while He was here on earth were certainly poor in
comparison with the solid-gold streets of heaven.

GET RID OF RELIGION

People often refer to wealth as if it, in itself, is an ungodly
thing. But money *in itself* is neither good nor bad. It takes people
to make money good or bad. People give money its value and
make it evil or good by how they use it. As we've already said, it
isn't having money or wealth that will keep you out of the
kingdom of God. It's *trusting* in money rather than in God that
will interfere with your service to Him.

When Jesus shed His precious blood, He redeemed us from
poverty, sickness and spiritual death. We seem to have no difficulty
in seeing that God is not balanced when it comes to being saved.

We can easily agree that salvation is for everyone all the time. And now we have come to a greater understanding about healing and can usually agree that healing belongs to everyone as well.

But when it comes to prosperity, all of a sudden we have to have "balance" about that. Why? Well, our arguments are not very well-founded. They usually go something like this:

"Now prosperity is a little bit different. You have to be careful telling people God wants them to have money and be prosperous. After all, so-and-so (usually naming some preacher) fell because of money."

Unfortunately, these folks are as serious as they can be without realizing how ridiculous it is to base what you believe on a backslidden preacher. Why would you follow or use as an example someone who has fallen into sin? You have to base your theology on what the Bible says, never on anyone's experience.

When it comes to being saved, you wouldn't follow someone who was backslidden. If someone decided he or she was not going to get healed, I hope you wouldn't follow that person. Then why, in the case of prosperity, would we base our theology on something that goes contrary to everything else we know about God? I'll tell you why. *Because it lines up with our religion.* It lines up with all the worn-out religious traditions we've heard all our lives.

But we need to get rid of those worn-out religious ideas. Remember, Jesus said you make **the word of God of none effect through your tradition** (Mark 7:13).

All the things you may have heard that glorify poverty didn't come from the Bible; they came from religion—dead, dry religion. If traditional religious teachers do use the Bible to back up their arguments, they usually pull some Scripture out of context and try to make it say something it doesn't say. These teachers may be well-meaning people, but wrong is still wrong. Such teaching is still a distortion of the Word of God.

If you've got any dead religion in you, I hope you get it out by the time you are finished reading this book! By that time you should know, if you don't already, that God is no more balanced about prosperity than He is about salvation or healing. Being "balanced" isn't part of God's character. But you won't find out about God's true character from traditional religion. For that, you have to get to know Him personally by spending time with Him in His Word and by looking at His actions.

GOD'S CHARACTER

Do you know that you can get to know God just as you can get to know another person? It's true. You can get to know God so well that when someone says, "God did this or that," you can immediately know whether it is true or not just by the nature of the work. How do you get to know God? You get to know Him the same way you get to know anyone—by spending time with Him and by listening to what He says.

Since what God says is found in the Bible, you have to spend time reading the Word. But it's necessary to do more than read it. You have to learn to "rightly divide" the Word. Second Timothy 2:15 says,

> **Study to shew thyself approved unto God, a work-man that needeth not to be ashamed, rightly dividing the word of truth.**

The Living Bible renders that verse:

> **Work hard so God can say to you, "Well done." Be a good workman, one who does not need to be ashamed when God examines your work. Know what his Word says and means.**

Paul's point is that if the Word can be rightly divided—that is, *accurately* and *correctly* read and understood—it can be wrongly divided—that is, *inaccurately* and *incorrectly* read and understood. In order to be sure you are handling the Word accurately, you have to ask yourself, *Does this interpretation line up with what I know the Scriptures say about God?*

For instance, James 1:17 says,

> **Every good gift and every perfect gift is from above, and cometh down from the Father of lights, with whom is no variableness, neither shadow of turning.**

Now, that verse says very plainly that good things come from God. And we've already established that healing and prosperity are good things and sickness and poverty are bad things. So if someone says God gave you an illness or God wants you to be poor, those statements contradict the Word of God, don't they? Since we know from the Bible that God is a good God who wants to give good gifts to His children (Matt. 7:11), we would be wrongly dividing the Word if we said He wanted us to be sick or poor. Saying that would contradict what we know about God's true character.

GOD'S ACTIONS

Another way to get to know God is to look at how He does things. We can understand a lot about God's attitudes toward us by observing His actions, not only in the Bible but also in the world around us.

For example, we often hear these days that the planet we live on is wearing out and running out of basic resources. We hear things like the statement I heard recently on a news broadcast's special report which said the earth is running out of trees. But if you believe that, you don't really know what is going on. My wife and I fly approximately 100,000 miles a year all over the world, and you can look out the window of the plane almost anywhere in the world, and all you see is trees. And no one is even living there most of the time.

You will hear that we are running out of land, out of space for people to live in, and that the earth is so overpopulated that there isn't enough food to feed everyone. But do you know that you can put all six billion people on planet earth in one state in the United States? And as for having enough food, do you realize there are so many fish in the oceans that we could all eat fish three times a day every day and there would still be so many fish that we couldn't catch them all? We would never run out of food if we ate nothing but fish, and that doesn't even count the produce of all the farms in the world.

So all this preaching about scarcity is unscriptural. The Bible says God created the earth, gave it to us to live in and promised to supply all our needs. (Phil. 4:19.) Do you think God made a mistake and didn't make enough stuff for us down here? Even though we don't always practice good stewardship of the resources God put in the earth for our use, there is more than enough of everything.

That is how God does things. God is a God of abundance, not a god of scarcity. But they won't tell you that on the evening news. And unfortunately, a lot of preachers won't tell you that either. You have to get to know God for yourself and find out what He is really like from the Bible.

LAUNCH OUT INTO THE DEEP

If you doubt that God is a God of abundance, just look at what happened to Peter in Luke 5. Remember what happened when Peter let Jesus use his boat for a pulpit from which to preach a sermon.

Now when he had left speaking, he said unto Simon, Launch out into the deep, and let down your nets for a draught. And Simon answering said unto him, Master, we have toiled all the night, and have taken nothing: nevertheless at thy word I will let down the net. And when they had this done, they inclosed a great multitude of fishes: and their net brake. And they beckoned unto their partners, which were in the other ship, that they should come and help them. And they came, and filled both the ships, so that they began to sink.

Luke 5:4-7

Just look what happened! They caught so many fish that the net broke and the boats began to sink. Didn't Jesus know the nets would break? Didn't He know He was giving Peter and his partners so many fish that their boats would be swamped? Of course He did, but He just couldn't help it! Overloading people with blessings is just His nature. It's just the way He does things.

Of course, in order to receive the abundance of God, Peter had to do what Jesus told him to do. He had to forget about his way of doing things. He had to forget what experience and tradition told him about how to fish in the lake he'd grown up fishing in. He had to forget about the "what ifs" and the "yeah buts" and totally rely on Jesus. But when he did that, God poured him out a blessing he literally didn't have room enough to contain.

Since Jesus is **the same yesterday, and to day, and for ever** (Heb. 13:8), He wants to do the same things for us that He did for Peter. He was a God of abundance for Peter, and He wants to be a God of abundance—an "over-the-top" kind of God—for you too. And He will be if He can talk you into letting Him. But you'd better get ready. When God starts unloading blessings on you, your boat may start to sink!

GOD'S NATURE

It's necessary for us to know what the Bible says God's true nature is so that we won't be afraid to approach Him. If you are going to ask God for something, you should at least know your odds of receiving an answer before you go in. You should at least know God's track record and how He has dealt with people in the past. After all, you know from experience that before you go in and ask your boss or your parents for something, you often have to get them in the right mood to receive you.

Is God the same way? Do I have to get Him in a good mood before I ask Him for what I need? What if I have done something recently that wasn't so good? What if I've even sinned? Of course I have repented, but does there need to be a cooling off period before I can go back to Him? We often treat God as if He is some kind of grouch who is out to get us, but let's look at what the Bible says about Him.

GOD GIVES RICHLY

One thing the Bible says about God, which is important for you to know if you are going to approach Him, is that He gives *richly.*

Charge them that are rich in this world, that they be not highminded, nor trust in uncertain riches, but in the living God, who giveth us richly all things to enjoy.

1 Timothy 6:17

The Amplified Bible says God not only **richly** gives to us, but He **ceaselessly provides us with everything for [our] enjoyment.** How does God give to us? According to the Bible, He gives to us richly and ceaselessly. That doesn't sound like Someone whom you have to get in a good mood before you dare asking for something, does it? God is such a giver that He does it richly and ceaselessly.

GOD GIVES FREELY

The Bible also says God gives to us *freely.*

He that spared not his own Son, but delivered him up for us all, how shall he not with him also freely give us all things?

Romans 8:32

To me this is one of the most reassuring verses in the Bible. Just imagine—Paul says God will *freely* give us *all* things. How did He prove it? He gave us Jesus.

He who did not withhold or spare [even] His own Son but gave Him up for us all, will He not also with Him freely and graciously give us all [other] things?

Romans 8:32 AMP

Don't you love that? God will not withhold anything from us. And His free gift is not based on our performance or on what we deserve, but on His character. God gives to us freely, not because of who we are, but because of who He is.

GOD GIVES LIBERALLY

Not only does God give richly and freely, but He also gives *liberally.* Look at the way the apostle James says God gives.

If any of you lack wisdom, let him ask of God, that giveth to all men *liberally, and upbraideth not;* and it shall be given him.

James 1:5

If any of you is deficient in wisdom, let him ask of the giving God [Who gives] to everyone *liberally and ungrudgingly, without reproaching or faultfinding,* and it will be given him.

James 1:5 AMP

Aren't you glad God isn't a faultfinder! When you approach God, He doesn't reproach you or recite a long list of the things you've done wrong before He answers your prayer. And He doesn't give to you grudgingly. He gives liberally. **He generously**

bestows His riches upon all who call upon Him [in faith]
(Romans 10:12 AMP).

GOD IS A REWARDER

It is also God's nature to give rewards. Hebrews 11:6 calls Him a **rewarder of them that diligently seek him.** That's the kind of God He is. He is a rewarder who gives liberally without finding fault. He ceaselessly provides for us richly. He gives to us freely and does not withhold from us.

All these Scriptures are good to meditate on anytime, but they are especially useful when you need to get in faith in any area. Before you can come to God with confidence, you have to know what kind of God He is. God is good all the time. He wants us to know Him as He truly is, to know His true nature, so He can bring us up to the level He meant for us to walk in. According to the Bible, we have been living far below our privileges as members of the body of Christ for too long.

UP TO ANOTHER LEVEL

Why do you think God gave man the technology for airplanes? Did He do it just for the devil and his crowd? Of course not. He gave it for His children and for the spreading of the gospel.

Or why did God give us the technology for television? Was it just for the world and all their pleasures? Of course not. God gave us television for the spreading of the gospel.

However, we have lived so far below our privileges for so long that we criticize a preacher for buying an airplane but never say a word about company executives who fly around in their own jets. And we criticize so-called "television evangelists" for saying where their next conventions or gospel meetings are going to be, but we never say a word about commercials that are trying to sell us stuff we don't need.

Do you see how messed up our thinking has been? Instead of buying something you've seen advertized on television, you ought to find a ministry that is trying to buy an airplane and send them some money!

Folks, it's time for us to come up to another level of thinking, another level of believing and another level of walking. It's time we walked on the level God intended for us to walk on all along. It's time we began to see God the way He really is—not the way the world has described Him, but the way the Bible describes Him.

God is good all the time. He is not balanced. He is completely one-sided and extreme about how He wants to bless you. When God thinks of you, He is thinking, *What can I do for my child that will just bless his or her socks off?*

It's the very nature of God to be a giver. If you don't know God as *Giver,* you don't know Him at all. God is a giver because He is a lover. It's the nature of love to want to give.

For God so *loved* the world, that he *gave* his only begotten Son, that whosoever believeth in him should not perish, but have everlasting life.

John 3:16

chapter three

CHANGE YOUR SAYING

The first and most important thing we have to do to begin walking in the abundance that God intended for us to walk in is to change the words that come out of our mouths. Yes, that's right. Biblical prosperity begins in your mouth. Healing begins, not in your body, but in your mouth with the words that you say.

Now, if you're new to the idea of biblical prosperity and haven't heard much preaching on the subject, you may be a little confused about this business of what is generally called "confession." If you have recently come out of a denominational background, you may have been taught to think confession just means confessing your sins to God or acknowledging them to another Christian. Or you may think it means making a public "confession" of your faith in Jesus Christ as your Lord and Savior when you join a church.

And of course, confession does include these things. But as you've probably discovered from your own experience and from reading the first two chapters of this book, just confessing your sins and even confessing Jesus Christ as Lord isn't enough to bring you into the prosperity and divine health Jesus bought for us on the cross. Confessing Jesus as Lord is enough to get you saved, and as we've said all along, that's the first and most important part of the threefold redemption Jesus paid for with His blood. But if we are to walk every day in the other two-thirds of our redemption, we have to do more than make a one-time confession of faith.

If we are to walk and live in the prosperity and health Jesus died to give us, we must make every word that we say line up with the Word of God.

And that means we may have to retrain ourselves completely. It means that many phrases we've been using all our lives— phrases like "I can't afford it" and "I've got the flu"—have to be thrown out of our vocabularies for good. If you are going to move into God's plan of abundance, you just can't say things like that anymore. But since most of us have gotten in the habit of speaking negatively, we have to make a conscious effort to change what we say.

THAT'S NOT EASY!

I didn't say it was easy! But it's not as hard as we sometimes act like it is. We tend to think—and even experts will tell us—that it takes years to change things, but actually all it takes is a decision. *You can change what you are saying in an instant.*

Now, I realize there are processes that we have to go through on some things, but I think we often use that as an excuse for not making the changes we know we need to make in our lives. We make excuses like, "Well, you know, I've been saying this all my life, so it is going to take some time to change it." Or, "It took a long time for me to get in this shape, and it will take a long time to get out of it."

That may be true in the natural, but I'm talking about a supernatural process here. There's nothing supernatural about changing over a process of time. Even the world can do that. But as believers we don't have to be limited to the natural. Why not get the supernatural involved? You got saved in an instant, didn't you? Salvation wasn't a process. One second you were a sinner on your way to hell, and the next second you were a saint gloriously saved and on your way to heaven. Salvation is the biggest miracle of all. And if it can be done in a moment, you can use your faith and your words to make other changes happen in a moment, too.

However, in order to change all your negative confessions into faith confessions, you need to know something about the nature of words and what the Bible says about the relationship between faith and confession. That's what I'm going to talk about in the remainder of this chapter.

THE SACRIFICE OF PRAISE

The Bible says in a number of places that we should open our mouths and lift up our voices to praise God. And yet after being in music ministry for twenty years, I know firsthand that praising God with the words of their mouths is one of the hardest things to get Christians to do. It's difficult, I think, because most Christians don't understand what they are really doing when they're praising God. They don't understand what the Bible means by a "sacrifice of praise."

**By him therefore let us offer the sacrifice of praise
to God continually, that is, the fruit of our lips giving
thanks to his name.**

Hebrews 13:15

Just what does this verse mean? How can praising God
with words be a sacrifice? To find out, we have to take a look
at the background of the Hebrew Christians to whom this letter
was written.

You see, the Hebrew Christians understood some things
about sacrifices that we don't understand in our culture today.
They knew that when they came into the presence of God in the
Old Testament, they had to come with a sacrifice. They couldn't
enter God's presence unless they brought with them an animal
for a sacrifice. And that animal, which was to be presented to
God as their substitute, as their representative, had to be the very
best animal they had.

However, the Hebrew Christians also knew they were living
under a new and better covenant established on better promises
(Heb. 8:6) than they'd had under the old covenant. And they
knew that the new covenant (or New Testament) said Jesus
Christ was **the Lamb slain from the foundation of the
world** (Rev. 13:8) who shed His blood once and for all to
redeem all mankind. Therefore, we don't have to offer any more
animal sacrifices, because Jesus Himself is the sacrifice.

**For Christ is not entered into the holy places made
with hands, which are the figures of the true; but into
heaven itself, now to appear in the presence of God for
us: Nor yet that he should offer himself often, as the
high priest entereth into the holy place every year with**

blood of others; For then must he often have suffered since the foundation of the world: but now once in the end of the world hath he appeared to put away sin by the sacrifice of himself. And as it is appointed unto men once to die, but after this the judgment: So Christ was once offered to bear the sins of many; and unto them that look for him shall he appear the second time without sin unto salvation.

By the which will we are sanctified through the offering of the body of Jesus Christ once for all.

But this man, after he had offered one sacrifice for sins for ever, sat down on the right hand of God; From henceforth expecting till his enemies be made his footstool. For by one offering he hath perfected for ever them that are sanctified.

Hebrews 9:24-28;10:10,12-14

Because Jesus made the blood sacrifice for all of us, we don't have to bring an animal sacrifice when we come into the presence of God the way worshippers did under the Old Testament law. Aren't you glad you don't have to take a lamb with you every Sunday when you go to church! However, that doesn't mean we don't have to bring something to sacrifice to God. Under the old covenant, God required an animal sacrifice, but under the new covenant, *what He asks for from us are words.*

ENCOURAGEMENT IN THE LORD

That's right—words. According to the Bible, the very best things that you can bring God when you come into His presence are words. And of course, the very best words you can bring someone are words of love and praise and honor and thanksgiving.

49

You would think that praising God would be the easiest thing for us to do. But it's amazing how many times when I ask a congregation to lift up their voices to praise God, I see them looking around helplessly after two or three seconds. They've said a couple of "Hallelujah's" and "Praise the Lord's" but can't seem to think of anything else. It's not that they don't want to praise God; they just don't know how to do it.

Well, one of the best ways is to do what David did in 1 Samuel 30. David was in a tough spot, and the Bible says he **encouraged himself in the Lord** (v. 6).

> **And it came to pass, when David and his men were come to Ziklag on the third day, that the Amalekites had invaded the south, and Ziklag, and smitten Ziklag, and burned it with fire; And had taken the women captives, that were therein: they slew not any, either great or small, but carried them away, and went on their way.**
>
> **So David and his men came to the city, and, behold, it was burned with fire; and their wives, and their sons, and their daughters, were taken captives. Then David and the people that were with him lifted up their voice and wept, until they had no more power to weep. And David's two wives were taken captives, Ahinoam the Jezreelitess, and Abigail the wife of Nabal the Carmelite. And David was greatly distressed; for the people spake of stoning him, because the soul of all the people was grieved, every man for his sons and for his daughters: but David encouraged himself in the Lord his God. And David said to Abiathar the priest, Ahimelech's son, I pray thee, bring me hither the ephod. And Abiathar brought thither the ephod to David. And David inquired at the Lord, saying, Shall I**

pursue after this troop? shall I overtake them? And he answered him, Pursue: for thou shalt surely overtake them, and without fail recover all.

1 Samuel 30:1-8

It's easy to see why David was deeply depressed in this situation. Not only had his camp been burned by the enemy and all the women and children kidnapped and all his supplies stolen, but his own men were blaming him for the disaster. No wonder he was deeply distressed.

However, he wouldn't allow himself to stay down. He didn't moan and groan and wring his hands and say, "I don't know what I'm going to do. I guess I need to go get some counseling from the pastor." No, he didn't do that.

What do you think he did? He encouraged himself in the Lord. He started reminding himself of all the things that God had brought him through. He reminded himself of the lion and of the bear.

And David said unto Saul, Thy servant kept his father's sheep, and there came a lion, and a bear, and took a lamb out of the flock: And I went out after him, and smote him, and delivered it out of his mouth: and when he arose against me, I caught him by his beard, and smote him, and slew him. Thy servant slew both the lion and the bear: and this uncircumcised Philistine shall be as one of them, seeing he hath defied the armies of the living God. David said moreover, The Lord that delivered me out of the paw of the lion, and out of the paw of the bear, he will deliver me out of the hand of this Philistine....

1 Samuel 17:34-37

Do you see what David was doing? Before he had gone out to fight Goliath, he had encouraged himself by rehearsing his past victories. He knew God had helped him in the past, and he relied on God to bring him through to victory in the present crisis. And that's what he did at Ziklag. He reminded God of all the things He had brought him through. And he praised God for who He is. Perhaps he used words like those in Psalm 8:

O Lord our Lord, how excellent is thy name in all the earth! who hast set thy glory above the heavens. Out of the mouth of babes and sucklings hast thou ordained strength because of thine enemies, that thou mightest still the enemy and the avenger. When I consider thy heavens, the work of thy fingers, the moon and the stars, which thou hast ordained; What is man, that thou art mindful of him? and the son of man, that thou visitest him? For thou hast made him a little lower than the angels, and hast crowned him with glory and honour. Thou madest him to have dominion over the works of thy hands; thou hast put all things under his feet: All sheep and oxen, yea, and the beasts of the field; The fowl of the air, and the fish of the sea, and whatsoever passeth through the paths of the seas. O Lord our Lord, how excellent is thy name in all the earth!

Psalm 8:1-9

Jesus quoted the second verse of this psalm as a prophecy of the praise He would receive: **Yea; have ye never read, Out of the mouth of babes and sucklings thou hast perfected praise?** (Matt. 21:16). David knew praising God would encourage him in his difficulty. And it worked, didn't it? Instead of sitting around in despair, David and his men pursued the Philistines and recovered all that had been stolen.

So the next time you're in a tough spot, come into God's presence with a sacrifice of praise. Praise God out loud and thank Him for what He's already done for you. Then begin thanking Him for what He's doing right now. And thank Him for what He's going to do in your life in the future.

OUR MAGNIFYING GLASS

Why is it so important to offer God a sacrifice of praise? Why are the words of our mouths so important? They are important because our mouths magnify every word we say.

That's right. *Your mouth is your magnifying glass.* Good or bad, whatever you talk about, you are magnifying. And so, when you praise God, you are magnifying Him. Your spoken or sung words of praise act just like a magnifying glass you might put over the words on this page. In reality, the letters in those words aren't any bigger than they were before. They just look bigger to you. God is already big. But it doesn't do you any good for Him to be big if He doesn't look big to you. How do you make Him look big to you? You magnify Him with the words of your mouth.

DON'T MAGNIFY THE DEVIL

But the trouble is that if you can magnify God with your words, you can also magnify the devil the same way. That's why it's so important to say the right thing. Have you ever noticed how when people talk all the time about their sickness, it gets worse? Or have you noticed how often people say, "I have [this or that disease]"? When you say, "I have it," that's the same as signing the receipt for it. It's yours because you claimed it. The devil will put symptoms and circumstances in your way, and if he can get you to say, "I have it," it's just as good as done.

So don't magnify with your mouth what the devil is doing. If you get up in the morning feeling a little feverish, don't say, "Oh, oh, I've got the flu. My wife and all the children have been down with it, and now I've got it too." When those are the first words out of your mouth, you are lining up with the devil right away instead of lining up with the Word of God, which says that by His stripes you're healed.

The same thing is true of prosperity. When you say, "I can't afford that" or "I can't do that because I don't have the money," you are just helping the devil keep you in poverty. If you are going to walk in God's abundance, you have to speak words that agree with the Bible, not words that agree with the devil.

The devil may be trying to tell you that you can't afford to do something God has called you to do, but the Bible says that God will supply all your needs according to His riches in glory. (Phil. 4:19.) Therefore, if you believe the Bible is true, you can afford anything you need.

And as a matter of fact, you can even afford anything you *want*. The Bible says, **The Lord is my shepherd; I shall not want** (Ps. 23:1). You can afford anything because Jesus redeemed you from poverty by His own precious blood.

THE WAY TO RECEIVE

The words of our mouths are also important because confession is the means through which we receive the promises of God.

In fact, we had to say the right thing even to be saved. In his letter to the Romans, Paul tells us how to receive salvation.

That if thou shalt *confess with thy mouth* the Lord Jesus, and shalt believe in thine heart that God hath raised him from the dead, thou shalt be saved. For with the heart man believeth unto righteousness; and *with the mouth confession* is made unto salvation.

Romans 10:9,10

This is the Scripture most of us came into the body of Christ on. And it's the Scripture we use to lead others into the body of Christ. But you need to realize that whenever the New Testament uses the words *saved* or *salvation,* it's talking about your redemption. It's talking about the fact that you've been redeemed from poverty, from sickness and from spiritual death.

Therefore, if we had to confess the right thing with our mouths to be saved in the first place, why do you think it would be any different for everything else that belongs to us? If you have to say something with your mouth to obtain your redemption from spiritual death, why would you think you had to do something different to obtain redemption from sickness or poverty? The fact is that redemption from sickness and poverty is received the same way redemption from spiritual death is received: by confessing with your mouth and believing in your heart. And strangely enough, *the confessing part is more important than the believing part.*

Now, before you get mad and throw down the book because you think I'm downplaying the importance of believing, let's look at what Jesus said about the relative importance of faith and confession.

THE FRUITLESS FIG TREE

Mark 11 tells the story of what Jesus did to a fig tree which should have had fruit on it but didn't.

And on the morrow, when they were come from Bethany, he was hungry: And seeing a fig tree afar off having leaves, he came, if haply he might find any thing thereon: and when he came to it, he found nothing but leaves; for the time of figs was not yet. And Jesus answered and said unto it, No man eat fruit of thee hereafter for ever. And his disciples heard it. And in the morning, as they passed by, they saw the fig tree dried up from the roots. And Peter calling to remembrance saith unto him, Master, behold, the fig tree which thou cursedst is withered away. And Jesus answering saith unto them, Have faith in God.

Mark 11:12-14,20-22

Let's analyze this story to be sure we understand exactly what happened. Jesus and His disciples were heading into Jerusalem for the day, and Jesus, who was hungry, went over to a fig tree He saw in a field to pick some figs. However, He discovered that although the tree was covered with leaves, it didn't have any fruit on it.

The *King James Version* says the tree didn't have any fruit because **the time of figs was not yet** (v. 13). That makes it sound as if it wasn't yet the season for figs, but apparently that's not what was happening here. According to horticulturalists, when a fig tree has leaves on it, it should also have figs. *The Amplified Bible* makes that clear:

> **And seeing in the distance a fig tree [covered] with leaves, He went to see if He could find any [fruit] on it [for in the fig tree the fruit appears at the same time as the leaves]. But when He came up to it, He found nothing but leaves, for the fig season had not yet come.**
>
> **Mark 11:13 AMP**

So Jesus expected this tree to have fruit on it, but it had none. Therefore, He killed it. He killed the tree that wasn't bearing fruit. How did He kill it? With His words.

The next morning as they were again passing by on their way to town, the disciples noticed that the fig tree was dead. And they were astonished. However, Jesus didn't pay any attention to it. Why? Because as far as He was concerned, the death of the fig tree was old news. The tree hadn't looked dead until the next morning, but Jesus knew it was dead the minute He spoke to it. He knew that His words, **No man eat fruit of thee hereafter for ever,** had gone right to the roots of that tree and killed it.

GOD'S KIND OF FAITH

Jesus knew His words had supernatural power, but His disciples were astonished because they were looking at things in the natural realm. Peter was so shocked that he said, "Look, Master. The tree You cursed is dead! Can You imagine that?"

The reply Jesus gave Peter was almost a rebuke. The *King James Version* doesn't give the correct translation of what He said in the original. Jesus didn't turn to Peter and say, "That's all right, Peter; if you just have faith in God, everything's going to be all right." That's not what verse 22 says in the Greek. In the Greek it says, "Have the *faith of God* or *God's kind of faith.*"

I believe Jesus was in effect saying to Peter, "If you had God's kind of faith, you would speak to things, and they would obey you too."

What kind of faith is God's kind of faith? We find an example of it in the very first chapter of the Bible. In twelve verses of Genesis 1 we find a recurring pattern or formula God used to create the universe. That formula was **and God said...and it was so** (Gen. 1:3,6,7,9,11,14,15,20,24,26,29,30).

Do you see the pattern here? God's kind of faith is the kind of faith by which you say something and then you see it come to pass. That's how God made everything He made. He spoke it into existence. And that's what Jesus was telling His disciples—"If you have God's kind of faith, you can speak things into existence too."

It would be an easy "out" for us if we had only this account from Genesis of God's kind of faith, because we could say, "Yeah, I know God spoke things into existence. But after all, He can do that because He's God. You can't expect us to do that, because we're only human." Yes, that's true. Genesis 1 was describing what God did, and we are only human.

But when Jesus cursed the fig tree and it dried up from the roots, He didn't do it as God. He did it as a man anointed by the Holy Ghost. Jesus operated on this earth as a man, not as God. When He came to earth, He laid aside His mighty power and glory and became a human being.

If you check the Scriptures, you'll find that Jesus didn't do any miracles or signs and wonders until He was anointed by the Holy Ghost. He was the Son of God His entire life, but there is no record of miracles until after He was baptized in the river Jordan and the Holy Ghost descended on Him.

That's why He said in John 14:12, **He that believeth on me, the works that I do shall he do also; and greater works than these shall he do; because I go unto my Father.** Jesus was saying that anything He could do, like speaking to a fig tree and killing it, we could do too when we have been anointed with the power of the Holy Ghost.

SAY, SAY, SAY

We know Jesus was telling His disciples that their faith was just as powerful as His, because He went on to explain it specifically.

For verily I say unto you, That whosoever shall *say* unto this mountain, Be thou removed, and be thou cast into the sea; and shall not doubt in his heart, but shall *believe* that those things which he *saith* shall come to pass; he shall have whatsoever he *saith*.

Mark 11:23

I want you to pay particular attention to the words I've emphasized in this verse. Notice that Jesus uses the word "say" three times and the word "believe" only once. Kenneth Hagin tells a story about how God brought this fact to his attention. He was holding a meeting in a town in Texas in 1951, and between services he was on his knees before the altar of the church, reading through the gospel of Mark.

When he got to Mark 11:23, the Lord spoke to him and said, *Did you notice that the word "say" is in that verse three times, and the word "believe" is in there only one time?*

Brother Hagin said, "No, Lord, I hadn't noticed that."

Then the Lord said, *You are going to have to do* three times as much *teaching and preaching about the "saying" part as you are the "believing" part to get people to see it. My people are not missing it primarily in what they are believing, but they are missing it in what they are saying.*

MISSING IT WITH OUR MOUTHS

Unfortunately, in spite of all the tools like cassette tapes, Christian television, teaching videos and Word of Faith books that we have available to us today that weren't available in 1951, many Christians are still missing out on a large part of their redemption. They've been taught about the believing part of faith, and they aren't missing it there. But they haven't heard so much about the saying part of God's kind of faith—or if they have heard it, they don't practice it—and therefore, they're missing it in what they are saying.

It's obvious that's where the problem is, because I still hear people say things like "I just believe God is going to heal me."

When they say that to me, I usually say, "Well, He's not! God has already done all He is going to do about healing you. He redeemed you from sickness 2000 years ago on the cross. That is what He did about your healing, and it is already done."

People sometimes say, "I'm just waiting on God."

He's waiting on you.

"Well, I just believe in His own sweet time..."

His own sweet time is right now!

As far as God is concerned, your redemption from sickness and poverty is already accomplished. However, receiving it is up to you. How do you receive it? With your mouth.

TALK TO THINGS

What did Jesus do to the fig tree? He spoke to it. He cursed it and killed it. Did you know that "things" can hear? This tree heard. Jesus spoke to a fever, and it heard Him and obeyed Him. (Luke 4:39.) If a fever can hear, a tumor or a cancer can hear. If a tree can hear, then money, which is made out of the paper that comes from trees, can hear too. We all know "money talks." Well, if it can talk, it can hear!

Notice that Jesus didn't talk to God *about* the fig tree. He spoke directly *to* it Himself. We spend a lot of time talking to God *about* things, but Jesus told us to talk *to* things. So if you want to change your financial situation, you need to speak to your finances just as Jesus spoke to the fig tree. You should speak to your bank account and speak to your debt. You need to call **those things which be not as though they were** (Rom. 4:17).

WHEN WE CHANGED OUR SAYING

I remember when my wife and I changed what we were saying about our finances. I have to admit that I used to say things like "I can't afford it" all the time. And if I had just stopped to analyze what was happening, I would have realized that the principle of confession was working for me the entire time. Jesus said we can have what we say. And I was having exactly what I was saying. I was saying I couldn't afford things—and I couldn't!

The irony of the situation was that some of the time I did have a good confession, especially when I was around the right people. When I was in a meeting with other Word of Faith ministers, I would line my mouth up with the Bible and say that God would supply all my needs. But at the same time, I thought that when I was at home talking to my wife about our finances, I had to be "honest and realistic" about it. I thought if I didn't say, "We can't afford to do this or that," I would be lying.

I wasn't being hypocritical. I just didn't have a revelation about the "saying part" yet. I didn't realize that faith and confession do not work if you only apply them part of the time. You have to keep your confession right all of the time—especially when you are at home talking to your wife about your finances. That is the most important time to be saying the right thing! When we finally got a revelation of that, we started saying things like "We have more than enough" and "Every bill is paid."

A CHECK IN MY SPIRIT

However, when we started saying, "Every bill is paid," not every bill was paid. Not by a long shot. We were saying we had more than enough, but we certainly didn't have enough right at that moment. In fact, we were approximately $100,000 in debt. We didn't know quite how we had gotten in that situation, and we didn't have any idea how to get out. The pressure was so great that I finally made an appointment with a bankruptcy lawyer.

Declaring bankruptcy was against everything I had ever believed, but I just didn't know where else to turn. When I walked into the lawyer's office, I got such a sick feeling in my stomach that I knew I couldn't go through with it. I knew that feeling was a check in my spirit and was the Holy Ghost quickening me.

Fortunately, I knew that feeling well, and I knew not to override it even though filing bankruptcy looked like the only way out of my financial difficulty. After all, my credit was already ruined anyway. Why not just walk away from all the debts and bills? Bankruptcy looked like the only choice. But as soon as I felt that check in my spirit, I turned to my wife and said, "I can't do it. I can't file bankruptcy. Let's leave." And the minute I said that, it was as if a two-ton weight lifted off my shoulders.

Of course, my wife was thrilled because she had been saying the whole time, "God can wipe it all out if we just get in faith about it." If I had listened to her in the first place, I wouldn't have had to go through all the misery I had gone through.

So we turned around and left the bankruptcy lawyer's office. I left that office with hope in my heart. That's all I had—just a little hope. But it was enough to get me started. And in almost no time at all, we were walking in faith and acting like the Bible is true. It is so good to follow the Holy Ghost. He was leading me by the inward witness. We changed what we were saying and saw God move miraculously on our behalf.

In a short time, we were overtaken by the blessings of God, not only to bring us out of this particular crisis, but to keep us in the future. Instead of saying what we had—debt and lack—we started saying what we expected to have—all bills paid and more than enough of everything. The Bible says you can have what you say. When we changed our saying to agree with the Bible, we received the blessings God wanted to give us all along. He had already paid all our debts on the cross. He was just waiting for us to receive our redemption from poverty by agreeing with Him instead of agreeing with the devil.

GOD MADE US RICH

God not only brought us out of a financial crisis, but He made us rich on top of it. When we were under all that debt load and pressure, I would have loved to just have the debt paid off. I would have given anything to be right at zero—because we were $100,000 below zero. But when God does something, He doesn't do it halfway. God not only brought us out of debt, but He blessed us far beyond what we had prayed for. And, of course, He did it supernaturally.

Some people who are still thinking in the natural see the blessings of God on us and say things like "Well, it was easy for you to get out of debt because you're a preacher, and people always give preachers money." Well, let me tell you, I had been in the ministry nearly twenty years, and no one was giving me money! Besides that, I know a lot more poor preachers than rich ones. Money doesn't come automatically to preachers just because they're preachers. Preachers have to use their faith for money just as everybody else does.

Another thing people would say is "Yeah, but you travel and do meetings with Kenneth Copeland; that's why you're rich." Folks, I was going in debt traveling with Kenneth Copeland. Now, that wasn't his fault. It was mine because I wasn't doing what he was teaching. But when I made the adjustment and started *doing* the Word, it started working for me. The Word only works if you work it. I had sat in meetings and heard ministers preach prosperity for years. I sat there and agreed with everything they said and shouted along with everyone else. But it never worked for me until I started *doing* it.

The Word will work for anyone who will work it. When I have preached this message in different places, we have gotten testimonies from everywhere from people who are being blessed. And not just ministers, but businesspeople, office workers, factory workers and professional people are seeing results. If the Word of God didn't work for any but a select group, what good would it be? But God is no respecter of persons. The Word works for everyone all the time.

NAME IT AND CLAIM IT

Am I one of those "name it and claim it" people? Do I believe in that "blab it and grab it" stuff? Am I one of those "confession" preachers like Kenneth Hagin and Charles Capps and Kenneth Copeland?

Absolutely!

But don't name "confession" preachers without naming Jesus. He was the biggest "name it and claim it" preacher of all of us. He's the One who started the whole thing. He's the One who spoke to things and made them obey Him and then told us to do the same thing.

If you came to tell me confession doesn't work, you came too late. I have already proved it out. I have proved you can change your life, your circumstances and certainly your finances if you start saying the right words. Psychologists say that if you tell a lie over and over, after awhile you will start to believe it yourself. Well, the same process will work with the truth.

My wife and I said over and over again that we were rich. Before long we started believing it was true, and sure enough, it came to pass. I heard Kenneth Hagin say recently, "Where you are and what you have today is a result of what you said and believed yesterday."

If you're not happy with where you are in life, maybe you should check to see if your situation is the result of wrong words coming out of your mouth. If you want to change your receiving, change your saying. Start speaking in faith to the circumstances you want to change, and then watch God pour His blessings out on you.

chapter four

CHANGE YOUR SOWING

Changing your sowing is another important key to unlocking the blessings of God in your finances. As we said in an earlier chapter, God's system of blessing His children financially is the direct opposite of the world's system. The world's system tells people to get all they can, to can (or store up) all they get and then to sit on the can. This is just a clever way of saying that in the world, people are told to acquire and store up as much money as they can. They then put this money in some safe place, hoard it and surround it with security systems so it won't be lost or stolen.

But God's financial increase system is entirely different. God's system is based, not on accumulation and hoarding, but on giving and receiving. And not only that, but God's system is one of abundance, whereas the world's system is based on scarcity.

Give, and it shall be given unto you; good measure, pressed down, and shaken together, and running over, shall men give into your bosom. For with the same measure that ye mete withal it shall be measured to you again.

Luke 6:38

This Scripture demonstrates God's attitude of abundance. To us, getting back **good measure** might seem to be enough. But God never stops just with enough. He goes on to *more than enough.* He gives us back not just **good measure** but **good measure, pressed down, and shaken together.** Now, even that seems like enough to give in return for a seed sown into His kingdom. But God doesn't stop there. He adds **running over.** He fills up your cup until it runs over. (Ps. 23:5.)

God always thinks in terms of abundance. Ephesians 3:20 says He wants to **do exceeding abundantly above all that we ask or think.** He wants you to have so much that you're not just full, but running over with blessings.

Full is only enough for you, but the running over part can go beyond your personal needs so you can help others. God wants you to have not only what you ask for, but more than you can ask for and even more than you can think of!

But just because God wants to fill up our cups to running over, or just because He is *able* to do it, that doesn't mean He does it automatically. As we've been saying all along, the blessings of God don't just fall on us without our doing anything to receive them. Notice that before it tells us what God will do, Luke 6:38 tells us what *we* must do. The first word of the verse is *give.* That tells us that *the way to get things in God's system is to first give things away.*

THE PRINCIPLE OF SOWING AND REAPING

Before we can harvest, we must sow seed. That is a principle of the spiritual realm just as it is a principle of the natural agricultural realm. Therefore, if you need money, you must first sow money; that is, you must give money. That's how God's system of sowing and reaping works.

The law of sowing and reaping is always in effect and works all the time in any area.

While the earth remaineth, seedtime and harvest, and cold and heat, and summer and winter, and day and night shall not cease.

Genesis 8:22

In Genesis 8, God promised Noah that He would never again destroy the earth with a flood. As part of that covenant, He also reestablished the law of sowing and reaping, or, as it is also called, the law of seedtime and harvest. God promised that as long as there is cold weather and hot weather, as long as there is summer and winter and as long as there is daylight and dark, there will be seedtime and harvest.

This law is one of God's principles which works regardless of whether we are aware of it. You don't have to confess it into working, nor can you do anything to stop it. Seedtime and harvest is a law of God which works all the time in any area.

Paul pointed out the absolute importance of paying attention to what you are sowing.

Be not deceived; God is not mocked: for whatsoever a man soweth, that shall he also reap.

Galatians 6:7

Everything you do is an act of sowing, and you will eventually reap a harvest of what you have sown. This is true of material seed as well as of spiritual seed. Whatever you sow is what you will reap. We know that's true in the natural, because when a farmer plants cotton, he always harvests cotton, and when he plants corn, he always harvests corn. It's the same way in God's system. Therefore, if you want to harvest money, you must sow—give—money.

This principle also affects the size of your harvest. If you want to increase, you have to give more. Jesus said, **With the same measure that ye mete withal it shall be measured to you again** (Luke 6:38). That means God will use the same unit of measure to give back to you that you used to give to Him. Paul reminded the Corinthians that **he which soweth sparingly shall reap also sparingly; and he which soweth bountifully shall reap also bountifully** (2 Corinthians 9:6). That's why the Bible says:

> **There is that scattereth, and yet increaseth; and there is that withholdeth more than is meet, but it tendeth to poverty. The liberal soul shall be made fat: and he that watereth shall be watered also himself.**
>
> **Proverbs 11:24,25**

Or as a modern translation puts it:

> **One man gives freely, yet gains even more; another withholds unduly, but comes to poverty.**
>
> **A generous man will prosper; he who refreshes others will himself be refreshed.**
>
> **Proverbs 11:24,25 NIV**

That's right. The Bible says a liberal, or generous, person will prosper and increase, but a stingy person will fall into poverty. We'll go into this principle in more depth later in this chapter, but first we need to be sure we understand the difference between *tithing* and *giving,* or *sowing.*

TITHING IS NOT SOWING

Most of us have a general idea of what tithing is. We know the Bible instructs us to bring the first tenth of whatever we receive to God.

Honour the Lord with thy substance, and with the firstfruits of all thine increase: So shall thy barns be filled with plenty, and thy presses shall burst out with new wine.

Proverbs 3:9,10

Bring ye all the tithes into the storehouse, that there may be meat in mine house, and prove me now herewith, saith the Lord of hosts, if I will not open you the windows of heaven, and pour you out a blessing, that there shall not be room enough to receive it.

Malachi 3:10

And here men that die receive tithes; but there he receiveth them, of whom it is witnessed that he liveth.

Hebrews 7:8

These Scriptures indicate that God will bless us when we tithe; however, we need to understand why tithing is not the same as sowing seed. Tithing is not sowing, *because the first tenth already belongs to God.* When you bring God the tithe, you are only giving back to Him what was already His. Therefore, it was never yours to sow. You cannot begin sowing until you have given God back what already belongs to Him.

Tithing puts you in position to begin sowing and reaping. You may think you can't afford to tithe, but actually, you can't afford not to. Let me ask you this: Can you afford to have God open up the windows of heaven and pour out on you such a huge blessing that you don't know where you are going to put it all? I'm sure you said yes! Well then, you must do what the Bible says to do in order to get in position to receive the blessing. Therefore, you must tithe.

If you really stopped to think about it, you would realize that your tithe is only ten cents. Anyone can afford to give God a dime out of every dollar. Surely you don't want a dime to keep you out of God's system of prosperity. After all, if you can't live on 90 percent of your income, you are not going to make it on 100 percent either. So be sure to bring God your tithe. If you don't, you are robbing God of what is rightfully His. (Mal. 3:8.)

A SENSE OF LIBERATION

There is such a liberation that comes when you begin giving offerings above your tithe. Giving above your tithe shows you, as well as God, where your heart is.

Lay not up for yourselves treasures upon earth, where moth and rust doth corrupt, and where thieves break through and steal: But lay up for yourselves treasures in heaven, where neither moth nor rust doth corrupt, and where thieves do not break through nor steal: For where your treasure is, there will your heart be also.

Matthew 6:19-21

Notice, Jesus didn't say that your treasure will be where your heart is. He said your heart will be where your treasure is. In other words, wherever you put your money is proof of where your heart is. If you put most of your money into your house, that is where your heart is. If you put most of your money into your car, that is where your heart is. *But* if you put most of your money in offerings for the spreading of the gospel, then that is where your heart is. No matter what you say, your checkbook will tell the truth.

WHEN WE MADE THE CHANGE

I remember well when my wife and I first began to change our sowing. Oh, in times past we had given offerings above our tithes, but since we had gotten into the financial situation I spoke of in the last chapter, it seemed to be all we could do to pay our tithe and still keep our heads above water. And we really weren't even doing that. So giving offerings seemed like the most financially impossible and irresponsible thing we could do. After all, we couldn't pay our bills. How could we give offerings?

But one night my wife and I were in a meeting where an offering was being taken. Sitting there in the pew, we were having a quick conference about how much we should give. I think we were trying to decide between giving five dollars and giving ten dollars. As we debated about it, something seemed to rise up on the inside of me that said, *This is not right.* And immediately, I turned to my wife and said, "Write the check for $100."

For us at that time, $100 was a huge amount. We were so far in debt that we had no idea how we would ever get out. We didn't know how our bills were going to be paid. But at that moment, we both sensed in the spirit that giving that $100 offering was the right thing to do. So we did it. And very soon we began writing $100 offering checks regularly. And then we increased to $500 checks, then to $1000 checks, to $2000 checks, and we've just kept going up from there.

And, praise the Lord, in almost no time we were completely out of debt. We're not really sure how it happened. No one gave us a big check to wipe it out; it just seemed to dwindle away quickly. The $100,000 debt, which had seemed to be such a huge mountain to us, was now removed and cast into the sea. All we had done was to change our saying and our sowing.

SEEK FIRST SOWING SEED

In Matthew 6:33 and in Mark 4:26, Jesus made two statements about the relationship of the principle of sowing to the kingdom of God, that is, to God's way of doing things. In Matthew 6:33 He said, **Seek ye first the kingdom of God, and his righteousness; and all these things shall be added unto you.** And in Mark 4:26, in His explanation of the parable of the sower, He compared the kingdom of God to a seed: **So is the kingdom of God, as if a man should cast seed into the ground.**

Since Jesus likened the kingdom of God to casting seed into the ground (sowing) and told us to seek first the kingdom of God, I don't think we are going wrong if we put those two statements together like this: "Seek ye first sowing seed into the kingdom." In other words, when you seek first sowing seed into the kingdom of God, He will see to it that things are added unto you. What things? The natural things like food and clothing that He was talking about in Matthew 6. Jesus said God knows we need material things to survive in our lives here on earth (Matt. 6:32), and God supplies these things in abundance when we sow seed first into His kingdom.

TURNAROUND

When my wife and I started seeking first sowing seed into the kingdom of God, our lives turned around. We had always had hearts to give, but we thought we didn't have the resources to give as we wanted to. But when we gave that first $100 check, there was great joy in our hearts. We didn't care anymore that we were living in a tiny apartment or that we had no car. We had gotten to the place in our lives where building the kingdom of God was the first thing on our minds and all we had a passion for.

And when we started operating financially out of that passion for God's kingdom, the windows of heaven opened up to us. We were blessed with houses and cars. Money and gifts came in with every mail delivery. It seemed blessings were overtaking us every time we turned around. We didn't seek them; they just came to us. We saw Matthew 6:33 come alive right before our eyes.

GOD'S WAY IS BETTER!

Whatever God brings to you is many times better than anything you could get for yourself. It is literally more than you can think of. For instance, if God hadn't led me there, I would never even have looked for a house in the neighborhood where we bought our first home. I just automatically thought, *We can't afford to live there.* But when God adds things to you, He does it better than you would do it yourself.

Another time, a certain man walked up to me in a meeting and said, "I want to buy you some suits." He told me where to go to pick them out, so I did. The bill came to several thousand dollars. Just one of those suits cost more than my entire wardrobe at the time!

The same week another man also said he wanted to buy me a certain brand of suit, and he wrote me a check for it. The check was for $3000!

I said, "What is all this money for?"

He said, "That's what that kind of suit costs."

I said, "Three thousand dollars—for one suit? I could buy a good used car for three thousand dollars!"

I couldn't imagine what a suit of clothes could be made of that would cost that much money. I knew I had to use the money for the suit since that was what it was designated for, but it certainly seemed like an extravagance. However, the man who gave me the money knew more about God's ways than I did. I'll never forget what he said to me.

He said, "God wants you to have the best."

That really hit me, and I immediately thought of "seek first sowing seed into the kingdom, and all these things will be added unto you." I didn't use my faith for that $3000 suit; I didn't even know a $3000 suit existed. That suit was just more of God's adding to me and doing it better than I could have done it myself. I wouldn't even have gone into that particular store to look at suits, much less thought about buying one there. But when we got busy seeking first sowing seed, God got busy adding things to us. And we have many more testimonies of the same kinds of blessings overtaking us.

AN ACCURATE SIGN OF PROSPERITY

Let me point out something here so you won't get your eyes off God and onto things. Where you live or what kind of car you drive or what kind of clothes you wear are not accurate signs of your prosperity. Remember, inner prosperity is more important than outer prosperity. Prosperity is *liking* where you live and what you drive and what you wear.

You certainly don't have to live in a big house to be blessed and prosperous. I know people living in big houses and driving luxury cars who are in debt up to their eyeballs and can't pay their bills. On the other hand, I know millionaires who live in apartments and drive old pickup trucks. God doesn't care where you live or what kind of vehicle you drive as long as you put Him and His kingdom in first place in your heart and don't allow yourself to get into bondage to things. God wants you to have the desires of your heart, and He wants you to have the best.

All these blessings God has given us have nothing to do with us or with who we are. They have nothing to do with my being a preacher. They came as a result of our getting our priorities straight and doing what the Bible says to do. When we started putting first the building of God's house, He started building our house. All we had to do was start to give. When God asks you to sow seed into His kingdom, He is not taking something from you. On the contrary, He is trying to give something to you. The blessing is not for His benefit but for yours.

Let's look at a story about a woman in the Old Testament which illustrates this point.

THE WIDOW'S LAST CAKE

And the word of the Lord came unto [Elijah], **saying, Arise, get thee to Zarephath, which belongeth to Zidon, and dwell there: behold, I have commanded a widow woman there to sustain thee. So he arose and went to Zarephath. And when he came to the gate of the city, behold, the widow woman was there gathering of sticks: and he called to her, and said, Fetch me, I pray thee, a little water in a vessel, that I may drink.**

And as she was going to fetch it, he called to her, and said, Bring me, I pray thee, a morsel of bread in thine hand. And she said, As the Lord thy God liveth, I have not a cake, but an handful of meal in a barrel, and a little oil in a cruse: and, behold, I am gathering two sticks, that I may go in and dress it for me and my son, that we may eat it, and die. And Elijah said unto her, Fear not; go and do as thou hast said: but make me thereof a little cake first, and bring it unto me, and after make for thee and for thy son. For thus saith the Lord God of Israel, The barrel of meal shall not waste, neither shall the cruse of oil fail, until the day that the Lord sendeth rain upon the earth.

And she went and did according to the saying of Elijah: and she, and he, and her house, did eat many days. And the barrel of meal wasted not, neither did

the cruse of oil fail, according to the word of the Lord, which he spake by Elijah.

1 Kings 17:8-16

Now, here was a woman whom God was trying to help. He was trying to save her and her household. However, He could only help her if He could get her to be obedient to the Word of God, so He sent the prophet Elijah to minister to her.

You might imagine that the first thing Elijah would do when he saw the woman he had been sent to help would be to offer something to her. But instead, the first thing he did was ask her to give him some water. Apparently, water was available, and she went to get him a glass of water right away. But then he asked for a piece of bread. And because she was down to her last measure of flour, his request for bread was a big problem for her. She didn't have enough to feed herself and her child, much less enough to give bread to an itinerant prophet who just showed up at her door. Since she was looking at her situation in the natural, she didn't see how she could afford to give away any part of her last piece of bread.

Most of us have been in this same situation. A "water offering" is what is easy for us—like the five- or ten-dollar offerings I was giving when I was so deep in debt. But then God sends a man of God around to ask for a "bread offering"—that offering of $100 or more that in the natural I didn't see how I could afford to give. I was in the same financial difficulty the widow of Zarephath was in and for the same reason: I had eaten my seed.

You see, this widow was about to eat the last piece of bread she had. She was about to consume the last thing she owned, which she could have used for sowing seed. And then she was going to die. That's what happens when you eat your seed. You die. Don't use your last five dollars to buy yourself a last meal—give that five dollars to God. Don't ever eat your seed. Sow it.

A THOUSANDFOLD RETURN

Elijah was not a greedy preacher trying to deprive a poor widow woman of her last meal. He was trying to get her to operate by faith in God's system of sowing and reaping. And fortunately, although she was hesitant at first, she finally did what he said. She obeyed the Word of God, which came to her by way of the prophet of God, and sowed seed by giving Elijah a piece of her last meal cake. When she did her part, God did what He had said He would do and provided abundant food for her, her household and Elijah for **many days** (v. 15).

What would have happened if this woman had not acted in obedience? She and her child would have died. If she hadn't sowed that last bit of meal as seed, she would not have had a harvest. If she had eaten her seed as she was planning to do, she also would have died just as she was planning to. But because she was able to trust God's Word and sow seed by giving Elijah a piece of bread, God was able to get a thousandfold blessing to her. A footnote in my Bible says the phrase "many days" means "a full year." Think of that! The widow sowed a seed that was actually only enough for one person for one day. But God gave her back enough for three people for one full year! That's not a bad rate of exchange.

SACRIFICIAL OFFERINGS

What Elijah asked the widow of Zarephath to give was a sacrificial offering. These days we don't seem to know what that is. A sacrificial offering is one you think you can't afford to give. I remember the days when someone would announce in a meeting that a sacrificial offering was going to be taken up, and the congregation would shout and praise God. But now people seem to be afraid to make sacrificial offerings.

Recently, I heard a minister say while taking an offering, "Now look in your bank account and see what you can really afford to give. Don't overdo it."

I wanted to jump up and scream, "Don't do it! Stop! The bridge is out! Don't go any further!"

Looking to see how much we can "afford" to give God is not what the Bible teaches us to do. That is what the world teaches us to do. If this minister had heard the prophet of God ask the poor widow in 1 Kings 17 for her last offering, he probably would have rushed over to her and whispered, "Don't do it, honey. You can't afford to give that. It's all you've got." And if she had listened to him, she and all her household would have died. She would have eaten her seed and stopped the growth process. There would have been no reproduction, and God would not have been able to save her life, to say nothing of blessing her with a thousandfold return.

If my wife and I had given what we could afford to give in the natural, we would never have made it out of our financial problems. In order to get out of the mess we were in, we had to do what the widow woman did and *give what we couldn't afford to give.* When God impressed me to give that $100, He was not trying to take $100 away from us. Rather, He was trying to get *$100,000* to us. He could never have done that if we had gone on eating our seed because we thought we couldn't afford to give it away.

THE SOURCE OF SEED

How do we get seed? By being sowers. The Bible says God will give seed to sow to those who are sowers.

> **Now he that ministereth seed to the sower both minister bread for your food, and multiply your seed sown, and increase the fruits of your righteousness.**
>
> **2 Corinthians 9:10**

If you see to it that you put first sowing seed into the kingdom of God, God will see to it that you have seed to sow. And not only that, but He will **multiply your seed sown.** Notice that God doesn't think in terms of simple addition. He thinks in terms of multiplication.

GIVING TO GET

Not long ago I visited with someone who said, "I think it is wrong to *give to get.*" If you think that, your thinking is wrong and out of line with the Bible. To think giving to get is wrong is like a farmer saying, "I am going to plant all this seed, but I don't want to get anything out of it. If I get a harvest, fine, but that is not why I am planting." Of course, no farmer would go to the trouble and expense of planting seed unless he intended to reap a harvest off that seed. And no one thinks a farmer is doing anything wrong when he plants a crop and expects a harvest.

Since God established the law of seedtime and harvest in both the natural and the spiritual realms, it is no more wrong for us to sow our money as offerings expecting to reap blessings than it is for a farmer to plant cotton seed expecting to harvest bales of cotton. Remember, we said earlier that the law of sowing and reaping works all the time in any area of life without our having to do anything about it. And it's only a traditional religious notion that it's wrong for us to line up with the principles God has set up to bless us.

Now, I'm not talking about giving with selfish motives, nor am I saying that every offering is a direct act of sowing for that purpose alone. There are times when we give just for the purpose of helping others who are in need, and we certainly should do that. We should give to organizations that help orphans, the homeless, the victims of disasters, the hungry and the sick. Jesus told us to help the poor. But in addition to these works of what we call "charity," you should find good ground to plant into on a regular basis.

SOWING IN GOOD GROUND

To be successful, a farmer must sow seed in the best ground he can find. If he plants in poor soil, his seed will not produce a large crop. In the same way, believers must find good ground to sow their financial seed into.

What is good ground? Basically, it's a work of ministry which is doing something to build the kingdom of God. Ministers or organizations are good ground if they are obviously bearing fruit for the kingdom of God. If a minister on television spends the entire program begging for money and saying things like "If you don't send us an offering, we'll have to go off the air tomorrow," they are not good ground. Why would anyone send money to a television ministry that is going off the air tomorrow? That would be the same as an investor deliberately buying stock in failing companies. You wouldn't tell your stockbroker to buy stock in a business that looks as if it may go broke in a few days. Well, if you wouldn't do that with an investment in the world's system, don't do it with an investment in the kingdom of God either.

You need to be very careful to whom and what you give your money, because when you sow money into something, you are hooking up with it. Hooking up with, or partnering with, people who know how to prosper in God can be the best thing that ever happens to you. Do you remember the enormous harvest of fish Jesus gave Peter in return for the use of his boat? That harvest didn't just benefit Peter; it benefitted his partners as well.

And when they had this done, they inclosed a great multitude of fishes: and their net brake. And they beckoned unto their partners, which were in the other ship, that they should come and help them. And they came, and filled both the ships, so that they began to sink.

Luke 5:6,7

When you partner with someone in your giving, you are hooking up with that person, and what is on him or her will get on you. Therefore, you'd better make sure that person has something you want. If I had been a fisherman in first-century Palestine, I would have liked to have been a partner with Peter. Being hooked up with Peter, I would have participated in his blessing.

The same principle still holds true today. My wife and I make sure that when we give offerings, we are sowing in good ground. We hook up with people who have something we need spiritually. We partner with people who walk in abundance, because we need to walk in abundance to fulfill the plan of God for our lives. What happens when we give to these people? The same blessing and the same anointing that is on them gets on us. We have associated with people who have hearts to reach the world, and now we have hearts to reach the world. Because we have helped them fulfill God's plan for their lives, God is seeing to it that we get the support we need to fulfill His plan for our lives and ministry.

KEEP IT GOING

It's important that you give to ministers and ministries that are givers themselves. When you give to people who are also givers, your seed never stops producing. We have partners who support us regularly, but that seed doesn't stop with us. In addition to going out preaching ourselves, we give to people who are reaching around the world with the Word. That way our seed and the seed of our partners never stops giving.

A minister I know related a story which illustrates the importance of not letting your seed be stopped or blocked somewhere. He said he felt led of the Lord to call several missionaries he was supporting and ask them, "Who do you give offerings to?"

One answered, "We don't give to anyone. We can barely make it ourselves."

The minister then said, "If you can't afford to be a giver, then I can't afford to sow into you."

At first, that may seem a little harsh, but it was exactly the right thing to do. I can't afford to have my seed getting blocked. When I sow my precious seed somewhere, I want to be sure it will keep going and keep producing for the kingdom of God.

THE MINISTRY OF GIVING

In his letter to the Christians at Rome, Paul said that we all have a ministry given us by God.

So we, being many, are one body in Christ, and every one members one of another. Having then gifts differing according to the grace that is given to us....

...he that giveth, let him do it with simplicity....

Romans 12:5,6,8

Verse 8 in *The Amplified Bible* says, **...he who contributes, let him do it in simplicity and liberality....** So a better translation of the word *simplicity* is "liberally." In other words, "Let him who has a ministry of giving do it liberally." Every believer has a part in the body of Christ. For instance, your little toe may seem to be an insignificant part of your body, but when you hurt it or lose it, you find out how important it is to you. Your little toe has much to do with your balance, and if it is not functioning properly, your entire way of walking will be affected. In the same way, all of the members of the body of Christ should be in their proper places, functioning as they were intended to.

Did you know that the proper function of some people in the body of Christ is to be givers? That is their high calling and their anointing. Of course, we are all to be givers, but some are set aside and called to the *ministry of giving*. There is an anointing to make money and disperse it into the Church and the ministry of the Lord Jesus Christ.

You might say, "That doesn't sound like a very spiritual function or calling." Well, that depends on how spiritual you think it is for people to get saved and make heaven and miss hell or how spiritual you think it is for a preacher or evangelist to go to another country, hold a meeting and see multitudes set free, healed and delivered. It takes money—and a lot of it, I might add—to go into all the world and preach the gospel to every person. (Mark 16:15.)

Therefore, there are people God has specifically raised up and called into the ministry of giving. Perhaps you are one of them. If so, get in your place and start fulfilling the call of God on your life. When you do, God will bless you **exceeding abundantly above all that** [you can] **ask or think** (Ephesians 3:20).

Remember, true prosperity is not as much about what you have as it is about what you give.

chapter five

THE WEALTH OF THE SINNER

In Proverbs 13:22, the Bible makes a statement which seems to confuse many Christians.

> **A good man leaveth an inheritance to his children's children: and *the wealth of the sinner is laid up for the just.***

What does the statement ***the wealth of the sinner is laid up for the just*** mean? It means exactly what it says. It means the wealth that sinners have accumulated actually belongs to the just, that is, to those who have been justified by the blood of Jesus.

"Now wait a minute, RayGene," you might say. "Doesn't that seem unfair to all the sinners who have labored for years and generations? Does that mean that all the wealth they have acquired is coming into the hands of the Church? If so, why would that be fair to them? Why would God do that to them if it was theirs to begin with? That sounds like stealing, and surely God isn't a thief."

NOT THEIRS TO BEGIN WITH

No, of course God isn't a thief, but in transferring the wealth of sinners to the Church, God is not taking away something they own. You see, the wealth wasn't theirs to begin with. We know God created the earth and everything in it, and everything God made, He made for His children. He did not make it for the benefit of sinners. He made it for the benefit of the just.

It's true that the devil has had the wealth of the earth in his possession for awhile, but, thank God, his lease is running out. That's the reason he is fighting the prosperity message so hard. He knows he is losing his stronghold in the Church. For years Christians have believed it is spiritual to be poor. Where do you think that idea came from? You're right—it came from the devil and the world's system, which he controls.

The devil's entire system is based on money and scarcity, but now that Christians are waking up to a revelation of what the Bible has said all along about prosperity and abundance, he is running scared. Therefore, he is busy stirring up as much dissension among believers as he can. Every second he can keep us preoccupied with our differences, another soul slips into his clutches. If we are going to rescue those precious souls out of the devil's control, we are going to have to have enough money either to go ourselves or to send someone else.

OUR RIGHTFUL INHERITANCE

The prosperity of the earth is rightfully ours because we are heirs of God and joint heirs with Jesus.

The Spirit itself beareth witness with our spirit, that we are the children of God: And if children, then heirs; heirs of God, and joint-heirs with Christ; if so be that we suffer with him, that we may be also glorified together.

Romans 8:16,17

Just look at what belongs to us as our inheritance. Since God made everything and we are His children, everything that belongs to Him also belongs to us.

The earth is the Lord's, and the fulness thereof; the world, and they that dwell therein.

Psalm 24:1

For every beast of the forest is mine, and the cattle upon a thousand hills.

Psalm 50:10

And he said unto him, Son, thou art ever with me, and all that I have is thine.

Luke 15:31

Why do we continue to think God wants believers to be poor when the Bible says God owns everything on the earth and what He owns also belongs to us?

THE GLORY EQUALS WEALTH

For further proof that the Bible is speaking of material wealth and not just spiritual wealth, let's look at what the book of Haggai says about the "glory."

...I will fill this house with glory, saith the Lord of hosts. The silver is mine, and the gold is mine, saith the Lord of hosts. The glory of this latter house shall be greater than of the former, saith the Lord of hosts: and in this place will I give peace, saith the Lord of hosts.

Haggai 2:7-9

Of course we know that the glory of God is the manifested presence of God. And we know the Lord is filling His house with

His manifested presence continually. However, sometimes the word "glory" is translated "wealth" or "riches" in various Bible versions. According to Hebrew scholars, one definition of *glory* in the Hebrew language is "wealth and riches." The reference to gold and silver in Haggai 2:8 supports that idea. In fact, the first time the word "glory" is used in the Bible it is referring to wealth.

And the man increased exceedingly, and had much cattle, and maidservants, and menservants, and camels, and asses. And he heard the words of Laban's sons, saying, Jacob hath taken away all that was our father's; and of that which was our father's hath he gotten all this glory.

Genesis 30:43;31:1

It's obvious that the "glory" referred to in Genesis 31:1 is the things mentioned in the last verse of chapter 30. The *New International Version, The Amplified Bible* and most other modern translations use the word "wealth" to translate the Hebrew word the *King James Version* renders "glory." We now have two witnesses from the Bible associating the idea of glory with wealth. Let's look at one more.

THE GLORY IS A SIGN

Isaiah also associates glory and material wealth.

Arise, shine; for thy light is come, and the glory of the Lord is risen upon thee. For, behold, the darkness shall cover the earth, and gross darkness the people: but the Lord shall arise upon thee, and his glory shall be seen upon thee. And the Gentiles shall come to thy light, and kings to the brightness of thy rising. Lift up thine eyes round about, and see: all they gather

themselves together, they come to thee: thy sons shall come from far, and thy daughters shall be nursed at thy side. Then thou shalt see, and flow together, and thine heart shall fear, and be enlarged; because the abundance of the sea shall be converted unto thee, the forces of the Gentiles shall come unto thee. The multitude of camels shall cover thee, the dromedaries of Midian and Ephah; all they from Sheba shall come: they shall bring gold and incense; and they shall shew forth the praises of the Lord.

Isaiah 60:1-6

In chapter 61, Isaiah further expounds on the same idea of the wealth of God's people as a sign to unbelievers:

And their offspring shall be known among the nations and their descendants among the peoples. All who see them [in their prosperity] will recognize and acknowledge that they are the people whom the Lord has blessed.

Isaiah 61:9 AMP

The subject of these verses is sinners being converted and backsliders coming home. Isaiah says that sinners and backsliders will see the glory of the Lord. But what kind of glory is the world looking for? People in the world don't discern spiritual things. They wouldn't know a "spiritual" manifestation of the glory of God if they saw it. However, they do discern the kind of glory the Word is talking about here. What kind of glory can they discern? Wealth. Riches.

Verse 2 says God will rise upon the Church and the world will see His glory upon us. Again, how will they see it? They'll see it manifested as material wealth and prosperity. They'll see that the wealth on the seas will be brought to you, to you the riches of the nations will come (Isa. 60:5 NIV). And they'll see gold and other valuable goods being brought to us from all the corners of the earth.

That certainly sounds to me as if a lot of the wealth sinners have been laying up is going to be transferred to the Church.

THE FIRST WEALTH TRANSFER

We need to remember that the end-time transfer of wealth from the world to the Church is not the first wealth transfer that has happened in the earth. Unfortunately, the first wealth transfer took place when man sinned and was driven out of the Garden of Eden. (Gen. 3:23,24.) In the beginning, God had given Adam and Eve authority over all that He had created. But when Adam committed high treason against God, Satan became the god of this world, and authority over all its wealth was transferred to him.

Because of this first wealth transfer, it seems today that most material wealth is located in the world's system. It appears that most millionaires and billionaires received their wealth in the world. And if this is true, how is the wealth of the sinner coming into the hands of the just?

FINDING ITS WAY

The Amplified Bible translation of Proverbs 13:22 says, **The wealth of the sinner [finds its way eventually] into the hands of the righteous, for whom it was laid up.**

Notice particularly the phrase **finds its way.** You and I don't have to make the wealth transfer happen. That is God's responsibility. Our responsibility is to seek first sowing seed into the kingdom of God, to keep our confession right and to **be not slothful, but followers of them who through faith and patience inherit the promises** (Heb. 6:12).

IT'S HARVESTTIME

There's plenty of evidence both in the Word and in what is happening all around us right now to show that the wealth transfer has already begun.

Ecclesiastes 2:26 says that God gives sinners **travail, to gather and to heap up, that** [they] **may give to him that is good before God.** This verse says plainly that people in the world are working hard and accumulating wealth so they can give it to the just. But why? Why would believers need all that wealth? Do we need it so we can all live in mansions and drive luxury cars?

No, that is not the reason. Of course, God is not against mansions and luxury cars, but the wealth that is coming into the hands of the body of Christ is to finance the gathering of the precious fruit of the whole earth, that is, the end-time harvest of souls. The wealth transfer we are talking about here is for the purpose of sending laborers into the Lord's harvest. (Matt. 9:37,38.)

However, let me assure you that if you start giving into the kingdom of God in a big way for the purpose of helping bring in this harvest, you will end up with houses and cars and lots of other stuff you never dreamed you could afford. Even the hose gets wet when water goes through it. If God can trust you to funnel money through your hands to finance the harvest, you will be so blessed that you won't be able to contain it all—**He that**

goeth forth and weepeth, bearing precious seed, shall doubtless come again with rejoicing, bringing his sheaves with him (Ps. 126:6).

YOUR PERSONAL HARVEST

The harvest is not just for the benefit of the corporate body, however. God not only wants to transfer wealth to the Church, but He also wants to bless you personally. God wants to overtake you with blessings. If you are consumed with His plan and with the end-time harvest, all these things will be added unto you. You really don't even have to use your faith for these blessings if you are seeking first sowing seed into the kingdom. Blessing is the plan of God for you, and if you are faithful to do your part, He will be faithful to do His. He will see to it that the wealth of the sinner finds its way to you.

chapter six

JESUS' ATTITUDE
ABOUT PROSPERITY

We often think Jesus was poor when He walked on the earth. In a sense He was, compared to what He left behind in heaven when He came to earth.

However, the New Testament makes it clear that Jesus walked in abundant provision in His earthly life and ministry. In the first place, He was wealthy enough to need a treasurer. And in the second place, His treasurer, Judas, embezzled money from the ministry treasury; but no one realized it, because there was so much money that they never missed what was stolen.

Let's look at some incidents described in the New Testament which show the attitude Jesus had toward prosperity.

FOOD FOR A CROWD

Of course we all know the famous story of the feeding of the 5000 with two fish and five loaves of bread.

Now the day began to decline, and the Twelve came and said to Him, Dismiss the crowds and send them away, so that they may go to the neighboring hamlets and villages and the surrounding country and find

lodging and get a supply of provisions, for we are here in an uninhabited (barren, solitary) place.

But He said to them, you [yourselves] give them [food] to eat. They said, We have no more than five loaves and two fish—unless we *are to go and buy food for all this crowd.*

For there were about 5,000 men....

Luke 9:12-14 AMP

What I want you to notice particularly is that the disciples asked Jesus if He wanted them to go into town and buy food for the entire crowd. That gives you a clue about how Jesus did things. Obviously, it wasn't completely out of the question for them to do that. Since His staff asked if He wanted to buy food for the crowd, we know Jesus must have provided for people through His own finances before. So we can assume there was enough money on hand in the treasury to at least consider taking 5000 people out to dinner.

Jesus chose to do a miracle to feed the 5000, but He made that choice for other reasons than not having enough money to do it in the natural. The Bible makes it clear that Jesus was walking in such abundant provision that He could have bought 5000 dinners if He had wanted to.

WORTH A YEAR'S WAGES

In another situation, Jesus proved that He was not concerned about saving money and economizing.

Six days before the Passover, Jesus arrived at Bethany, where Lazarus lived, whom Jesus had raised from the dead. Here a dinner was given in Jesus'

honor. Martha served, while Lazarus was among those reclining at the table with him. Then Mary took about a pint of pure nard, an expensive perfume; she poured it on Jesus' feet and wiped his feet with her hair. And the house was filled with the fragrance of the perfume.

But one of his disciples, Judas Iscariot, who was later to betray him, objected, "Why wasn't this perfume sold and the money given to the poor? It was worth a year's wages."

John 12:1-5 NIV

The perfume Mary poured on Jesus' feet was worth a year's wages. Biblical scholars estimate that in today's money a year's wages for an average worker would be about $20,000. That's a lot of money to pour on someone's feet!

Wouldn't you think that Jesus should have rebuked Mary for "wasting" something so expensive, something that could have been turned into so much money? But instead of criticizing Mary's action, Jesus praised it. In Mark's version of the story, Jesus said, **Let her alone; why trouble ye her? she hath wrought a good work on me** (Mark 14:6). Jesus was saying that prosperity is good, that abundance is good. Jesus pointed out that Mary had done what she could. (Mark 14:8.) She had given the very best she had to the Lord. As far as she was concerned, nothing was too expensive or too valuable to give to God.

Unfortunately, too many people I know say the same thing the disciples said: **Why was this waste of the ointment made?** (Mark 14:4). They say, "That is not being a very good steward of God's money. It would be better stewardship to use that $20,000 to help the needy instead of wasting it on one person."

I have heard people criticize Robert Schuller for spending millions of dollars on building the Crystal Cathedral. One of Dr. Schuller's critics said exactly what Judas said about Mary's "waste" of the expensive perfume: "Do you realize how many poor people he could have fed with the money it took to build that building?" This man was implying that Dr. Schuller took money out of God's "feed the poor" account and built an elaborate building with it—as if God wouldn't give him enough money to do both.

My friends, if you think that way, you don't know very much about God. He has more than enough for everything. Of course, good stewardship is important, but being stingy is not the same thing as being responsible with God's money.

We should be very careful not to criticize other Christians for being blessed financially by God. As Creflo Dollar said once, "Don't judge my harvest until you have seen my seed." You may see some people blessed to overflowing, but you don't know what they have done for God or what they have sown into His kingdom. Nor do you know what God may have called them to do. Just keep your attention focused on what God has called you to do and stay out of other people's business.

JESUS AND THE POOR

"But, RayGene," you may be protesting, "surely you're not saying Jesus was opposed to helping the poor."

No, of course I'm not saying that. And Jesus didn't say that either. As usual, what Jesus said was that we must keep our priorities straight.

> **The poor you will always have with you, and you can help them any time you want. But you will not always have me.**
>
> **Mark 14:7 NIV**

We know that what Jesus said here about the poor is as true today as it was 2000 years ago. There will always be poor people, and of course we should do everything we can to help them. However, the best thing we can do for the poor is not just to give them money to buy food and clothes but to help them with something eternal. Natural food may prolong their lives another day, but spiritual food will have eternal value both for them and for us.

Jesus understood the need for spiritual as well as natural food. Therefore, He said that a large part of His mission on earth was to preach the gospel to the poor.

> **The Spirit of the Lord is upon me, because he hath anointed me *to preach the gospel to the poor;* he hath sent me to heal the brokenhearted, to preach deliverance to the captives, and recovering of sight to the blind, to set at liberty them that are bruised.**
>
> **Luke 4:18**

> **The blind receive their sight, and the lame walk, the lepers are cleansed, and the deaf hear, the dead are raised up, and *the poor have the gospel preached to them.***
>
> **Matthew 11:5**

We know that the word *gospel* means "good news." Well, what would be good news to a poor person? "You don't have to be sick anymore"? No! That is good news to a sick person.

Good news to a poor person is "You don't have to be poor anymore." If you are poor or have ever been poor, you know that is good news.

ALL SHE HAD TO LIVE ON

Jesus also demonstrated His attitude toward prosperity one day when He was sitting in the temple watching people putting money into the offering.

And He sat down opposite the treasury, and began observing how the people were putting money into the treasury; and many rich people were putting in large sums.

And a poor widow came and put in two small copper coins, which amount to a cent.

Calling His disciples to Him, He said to them, "Truly I say to you, this poor widow put in more than all the contributors to the treasury; for they all put in out of their surplus, but she, out of her poverty, put in all she owned, all she had to live on."

Mark 12:41-44 NAS

Here Jesus is making the point that it isn't the size of your gift that is important to Him. What's important to Him is the size of your gift *in proportion to your wealth.* (Remember what we said in chapter 4 about sacrificial giving.) The rich people in the temple were giving what they could afford to give, but the widow was giving what she couldn't afford to give in the natural. She was sowing in faith everything she had.

Of course, the temple treasurers wouldn't be impressed with her penny. In the midst of all the offerings given by the wealthy, the widow's penny wouldn't be noticed. But Jesus noticed it and was impressed with it because He recognized her faith. He knew she was putting God first in her life, because she was giving a larger offering *in proportion* to what she had than the wealthy people were.

HOW MUCH IS LEFT?

The apostle Paul makes this same point.

For if the willingness is there, the gift is acceptable according to what one has, not according to what he does not have.

2 Corinthians 8:12 NIV

I have heard Dr. John Avanzini explain this verse like this: God is not so much interested in the size of your gift as He is in how much you have left after you give. If you give all you have, even if it is only a penny, God considers your gift larger than the gift of a millionaire who gives $10,000.

Naturally, the church is impressed by a $10,000 check in the Sunday offering and pays no attention to some loose change. But if those few coins were given by a struggling single mother who is believing God to provide for her in her poverty, God may view her gift as the largest offering in the plate. After all, the Bible says God does not look on outward appearances; God looks on the heart. (1 Sam. 16:7.)

PARTNERS IN THE GOSPEL

I think one of the reasons we have traditionally thought Jesus was poor is that He didn't seem to have an obvious source of income. He didn't have a job or own a business, and He didn't come from a wealthy family. Although He worked as a carpenter when He was growing up, He gave up that profession when He entered the full-time ministry. And on top of that, Jesus even called other men away from their jobs and businesses to follow Him. Yet it's obvious that Jesus and the disciples were abundantly provided for during His earthly ministry. Where did the money come from?

It came from the same place that the money to operate most modern ministries comes from—it came from His partners. Yes, that's right. Jesus had financial partners, people who had hooked up with Him financially to help Him fulfill the call of God on His life.

> **And it came to pass afterward, that he went throughout every city and village, preaching and shewing the glad tidings of the kingdom of God: and the twelve were with him, And certain women, which had been healed of evil spirits and infirmities, Mary called Magdalene, out of whom went seven devils, And Joanna the wife of Chuza Herod's steward, and Susanna, and many others, which ministered unto him of their substance.**
>
> **Luke 8:1-3**

It's apparent from these verses that there were wealthy people who were traveling with Jesus and using their money to finance the work of His ministry. Because it takes a great deal of money to travel around preaching the gospel, healing people and setting them free, God provided Jesus with many partners to minister **unto him *of their substance,*** that is, of their material wealth.

We don't have space here in this book to go into the subject of partnership in-depth, but I want to emphasize two things. First, it is scriptural to have partners. If you are called into the full-time ministry, you don't have time to work at a job on the side to provide your income. You may do that at first while you are getting started or are in training, but eventually God will insist that you give all your time to His business. He will provide you the money to do what He has called you to do, and one of the ways He does it is through partners.

Secondly, since it is scriptural for a minister to have partners, it is certainly scriptural to be a partner. Hooking up in financial partnership with the ministers and ministries that are feeding you spiritually is one of the major ways you can sow your seed. One of the functions of a ministry is to be good ground for believers to sow their financial seed into. The apostle Paul understood that. He wrote to his partners in the church at Philippi that he was glad they had sent him money, not because he desired a gift, but because he wanted them to have a harvest from their giving.

Now ye Philippians know also, that in the beginning of the gospel, when I departed from Macedonia, no church communicated with me as concerning giving and receiving, but ye only. For even in Thessalonica ye sent once and again unto my necessity. Not because I desire a gift: but *I desire fruit that may abound to your account.*

Philippians 4:15-17

Most "good ground" ministries I know about are also partners with other ministries and regularly sow a portion of their partners' seed into the work of the gospel through these other ministries.

Therefore, as we said in our discussion of the law of sowing and reaping, when you give to people who are also givers, your seed has the opportunity to be multiplied far beyond your wildest dreams. The blessings God pours out on your partners, He will also pour out on you.

SAVING THE BEST FOR LAST

On the third day a wedding took place at Cana in Galilee. Jesus' mother was there, and Jesus and his disciples had also been invited to the wedding. When the wine was gone, Jesus' mother said to him, "They have no more wine."

"Dear woman, why do you involve me?" Jesus replied. "My time has not yet come."

His mother said to the servants, "Do whatever he tells you."

Nearby stood six stone water jars, the kind used by the Jews for ceremonial washing, each holding from twenty to thirty gallons.

Jesus said to the servants, "Fill the jars with water"; so they filled them to the brim.

Then he told them, "Now draw some out and take it to the master of the banquet." They did so, and the master of the banquet tasted the water that had been turned into wine. He did not realize where it had come from, though the servants who had drawn the water knew. Then he called the bridegroom aside and said, "Everyone brings out the choice wine first and then the cheaper wine after the guests have had too much to drink; but you have saved the best till now." This, the first of his miraculous signs, Jesus performed at

Cana in Galilee. He thus revealed his glory, and his disciples put their faith in him.

John 2:1-11 NIV

Jesus was such a firm believer in supernatural prosperity and abundance that it shouldn't surprise us that His first miracle was one of abundant provision. And notice that it wasn't only the *quantity* of the wine that seemed miraculous; it was the *quality* of the wine as well. Instead of providing a couple of gallon jugs of off-the-shelf, commercial-grade wine, Jesus provided 150 gallons of vintage, estate-bottled wine. Just think what 150 gallons of imported French wine would cost today. And yet Jesus provided that much fine wine for the guests at a country wedding.

Jesus is the same today as He was when He walked the earth 2000 years ago. (Heb. 13:8.) And He is as willing to provide abundantly for us today as He was to provide the best for the wedding guests at Cana. I like what the governor of the feast said: "You saved the best for last." Thank God we are in the last days, and Jesus has saved the best for last. All we have to do is sow our seed and stand in faith for God's harvest. The best is yet to come.

chapter seven

NEW TESTAMENT PROVISION/
OLD TESTAMENT WEALTH

There seems to be a great difference in the provision we see in the New Testament and the wealth we see in the Old Testament. Although there are many New Testament Scriptures on prosperity, sowing and reaping and abundant provision, in the Old Testament we see wealth piled up on every side.

Why is that? If prosperity is for us today, why don't we have New Testament examples of that kind of wealth? Since we are New Testament believers, everything we believe should be based on the New Testament.

We studied earlier in the book about the wealth of the sinner that, according to the Bible, is laid up for the just. We found out there is an end-time transfer of this wealth. Over and over again we read how wealth is going to be transferred from the world into the body of Christ. Why doesn't the New Testament say more about this transfer, and why don't we see it happening in New Testament times?

THE CHURCH AGE

First of all, we need to realize that we are in the same dispensation that the first Christians were in during the New Testament times. We are the same Church, and we're in the same Church age. We call theirs the early Church and ours the "last-days" Church, but it is still the same Church.

The *end-time* wealth transfer had not yet taken place during the time of the writing of the New Testament. God did not design this wealth transfer for the beginning of the Church age—what the Bible calls the **former rain.** Rather, He designed the wealth transfer for the last days of the Church age, for the **latter rain** (Joel 2:23)—that is, for the end-time harvest of souls.

In order to understand this difference, let's look first at what the New Testament says about what belongs to us now and at the promises we should be standing on, studying, believing and confessing. Then we will go over to the Old Testament and look at what is coming to us when that end-time wealth transfer is in full force.

ABUNDANT PROVISION

But my God shall supply all your need according to his riches in glory by Christ Jesus.

Philippians 4:19

Philippians 4:19 is probably the most quoted prosperity Scripture in the Bible—and for good reason. If you have ever had needs that required supplying, this is the Scripture for you. Notice particularly what God uses for a measuring stick to determine the size of your blessing—His riches in glory! Thank God

He didn't say "according to the economy of the United States." You never know how good or bad that is going to be. The world's economy goes up and down, but God's economy is always stable. God's economy never fails, because it is based on the unceasing law of seedtime and harvest.

AN INCREASE IN CREDIT

In order to recognize Philippians 4:19 as a harvest Scripture, we have to go back a few verses and see what Paul was talking about. Starting with the fourteenth verse, we see that Paul was commending the Philippians for their giving, because they had sowed seed into his ministry.

> **Notwithstanding ye have well done, that ye did communicate with my affliction. Now ye Philippians know also, that in the beginning of the gospel, when I departed from Macedonia, no church communicated with me as concerning giving and receiving, but ye only. For even in Thessalonica ye sent once and again unto my necessity. Not because I desire a gift: but I desire fruit that may abound to your account. But I have all, and abound: I am full, having received of Epaphroditus the things which were sent from you, an odour of a sweet smell, a sacrifice acceptable, wellpleasing to God.**
>
> **Philippians 4:14-18**

Because the *King James Version* uses some words in ways that are a little old-fashioned, I'm going to translate some of these words into modern English.

The word *communicated* in verses 14 and 15 means "giving." And a better word for *affliction* in verse 14 is "lack." When we read the passage that way, we see Paul is saying, in effect, "You did well in giving to my lack. None of the other churches gave to me, but you did over and over again."

When he says **I desire fruit that may abound to your account** (v. 17), Paul means he wants them to have a harvest, and he knows the only way they will reap is if they sow. What if a farmer went out to his field at harvest season and tried to harvest the crop but had not planted anything in the field that year? There would be no harvest, because he hadn't planted.

The Amplified Bible paints a clear picture of the harvest for us.

...I...am eager for the fruit which increases to your credit [the harvest of blessing that is accumulating to your account].

Philippians 4:17 AMP

Every time you give, you are actually putting money into a heavenly bank account. The only difference is that the return God gives you is thirty-, sixty- or a hundredfold (Mark 4:20) instead of a mere 2 or 3 percent.

AN OFFERING PLEASING TO GOD

Paul then says something in verse 18 that should make you think a little differently about the seed you sow. He says it is a sweet-smelling sacrifice that is well pleasing to God. Isn't it incredible that we can give something that would be well pleasing to God? To Him, our gifts are not filthy lucre but are like a sweet aroma which pleases Him. Realizing that my offering is pleasing to God makes me want to give all the more.

After commending the Philippians for giving and sowing their seed, Paul then tells them about the harvest they can expect. Notice carefully that verse 19 is written to *givers*. Although everyone uses it, if you read this verse in context, you realize Paul is talking about supplying the needs of the givers to whom he was writing.

THE IMPORTANCE OF ATTITUDE

It's important for us to understand that it isn't only the gift that is pleasing to God; it is the *attitude with which the gift is given* that makes the gift pleasing to God. Paul explains the importance of attitude—both our attitude and God's—in 2 Corinthians.

[Remember] this: he who sows sparingly and grudgingly will also reap sparingly and grudgingly, and he who sows generously [that blessings may come to someone] will also reap generously and with blessings.

Let each one [give] as he has made up his own mind and purposed in his heart, not reluctantly or sorrowfully or under compulsion, for God loves (He takes pleasure in, prizes above other things, and is unwilling to abandon or to do without) a cheerful (joyous, "prompt to do it") giver [whose heart is in his giving].

And God is able to make all grace (every favor and earthly blessing) come to you in abundance, so that you may always and under all circumstances and whatever the need be self-sufficient [possessing enough to require no aid or support and furnished in abundance for every good work and charitable donation].

2 Corinthians 9:6-8 AMP

It's obvious that Paul is speaking here not about merely giving, but about an *attitude* of giving. The ground you sow your seed into—a church, a ministry, a missionary work—doesn't care whether you give your gift grudgingly or cheerfully. But God cares. God loves cheerful givers so much that He is unwilling to do without them. When believers really have a heart to give, God promises to pour out **every favor and earthly blessing** on them.

Notice, this verse doesn't say *heavenly* blessing. It says *earthly* blessing. Thank God, we can have our blessings while we are still here. After all, we won't need them in heaven. We need them while we are on the earth. God wants us to have not only enough, but enough to give—and not only enough to give, but enough to give generously to every work we have in our hearts to give to. That is God's will for each one of us.

MAKING A GIVING

"But where is all this seed going to come from?" you may be asking. "I work over forty hours a week now just to make a living."

Well, that's where you're making your mistake. The Bible doesn't tell us we should work to make a *living*—the Bible says we should work to make a *giving*.

> **Let him that stole steal no more: but rather let him labour, working with his hands the thing which is good, that he may have to give to him that needeth.**
>
> **Ephesians 4:28**

Does this Scripture say the former thief should work so that he may have money to live? No. It says he should work so he may have something to give!

You can work from dawn until dark and still not have enough to live on. But when you become a tither, you can go further on 90 percent of your income than you could on 100 percent. And when you begin giving above your tithe, the blessings will begin to overtake you.

I know this is true, because I have proved it out in my own experience. My wife and I used to try to make our living off of the offerings we received, but it was never enough. We couldn't pay our bills and were going into debt in a hurry. Then we changed our thinking and started to implement the principles I have shared with you in this book—and everything changed. We started to make our living from *our* giving instead of from the giving of the churches. And when we began believing God for a harvest off the seed *we* were sowing instead of simply eating the seed that other people sowed into our ministry, God opened the windows of heaven on us and started pouring out blessings on us at every turn. Now we don't work to make a living—we work to make a giving!

BEING A PARTNER

The first thing we did was to start partnering with certain ministries. It takes people partnering with ministries to advance the gospel. There are billions of people to be reached, and it will take billions of dollars to reach them.

As we saw in a previous chapter, partnering with a ministry is nothing new. Jesus had partners. Paul had partners; and to do their part in reaching the world, ministers today are going to have to have partners, other believers who will hook up with them financially to help them fulfill the call of God on their lives.

I said before that becoming a partner with a "good ground" ministry is one of the best things you can do. Of course, you should tithe to your storehouse. For most of us that is our local church. But you should also give above your tithe to other men and women who are preaching the gospel, and especially to missionaries and evangelists. God's heart is the precious fruit of the whole earth—that is, souls—and our hearts should be in the same place.

SUPPORTING MISSIONARIES

In fact, the Bible tells us to support missionaries.

For these [traveling missionaries] have gone out for the Name's sake (for His sake) and are accepting nothing from the Gentiles (the heathen, the non-Israelites).

So we ourselves ought to support such people [to welcome and provide for them], in order that we may be fellow workers in the Truth (the whole Gospel) and cooperate with its teachers.

3 John 7,8 AMP

There are some missionaries and ministries whose sole support comes to them through their partners. They preach in places and countries where offerings are not received. We should abundantly give to works such as these. When you give to support missionaries, you get credit for everything they do, because you had a part in it. Every healing, every miracle, every salvation gets credited to your heavenly account because you helped send them. Not all of us are called to go out into the field as missionaries, but we can all take part in the ministry of those who are called by sending them our financial support.

NEW TESTAMENT PRINCIPLES

You can easily see that there is much in the New Testament about sowing seed. Giving offerings is the avenue that leads a believer into divine prosperity. You can get money in other ways, but sowing seed is the way to open the door of divine prosperity. I have recently heard people teaching in the Church on ways to come up with witty inventions, and that is fine. Believing God for witty inventions is certainly scriptural—**I wisdom dwell with prudence, and find out knowledge of witty inventions** (Prov. 8:12).

I have also heard people say that we need to go to business classes and study the primary way the world is getting their money and do the same thing. I am not against any of those things. What I am talking about is something to add to everything else you are doing. No matter what else you do, you should be a sower. If you really believed the kingdom of God was the best ground to sow into, you would invest all your money there. I believe the kingdom of God is the best thing in the world to invest in.

God's financial system is a system of sowing and reaping. And to get Him involved in our finances, we have to get involved in His system. How is God going to transfer the wealth of the sinner into the hands of the just? Through the law of sowing and reaping. How is that going to happen, exactly? I don't know. But I do know this: If you do your part, God will do His part. When you do your part by sowing seed, He will do His part by bringing in your harvest.

OLD TESTAMENT WEALTH

The Bible says that believers under the New Testament have a better covenant based on better promises than did believers in the Old Testament. (Heb. 8:6.) Therefore, if many of God's people under the old covenant were billionaires by today's money standards and we live under a better covenant, it seems reasonable that God should have some billionaires today. In some cases, people under the old covenant had such huge wealth that they couldn't contain it all. Let's look now at some of these instances of wealth in the Old Testament in order to get a glimpse of what lies ahead for those who are sowers in the body of Christ.

ABRAHAM AND LOT

Abraham and his nephew Lot had so much stuff that they couldn't even live in the same part of the country.

> **Abram had become very wealthy in livestock and in silver and gold.**
>
> **Now Lot, who was moving about with Abram, also had flocks and herds and tents. But the land could not support them while they stayed together, for their *possessions* were so great that they were not able to stay together.**
>
> **Genesis 13:2,5,6 NIV**

Abraham and Lot had to split up because there wasn't enough grass and water to feed all their livestock. That would be like everyone in your neighborhood having to move out because you have too much stuff. And Abraham and Lot didn't just have a lot of stuff; they had a lot of *good* stuff. Besides silver and gold, they had many flocks and herds and tents—all the things which represented wealth in their day. In today's terms that would be like having cars, boats, houses, buildings and bank accounts bulging with cash.

Folks, that's the kind of wealth that is laid up for people in the Church who are sowers. Abraham was extremely rich, and if you belong to Christ, then you are Abraham's seed and an heir according to the promise. (Gal. 3:29.)

THE FAVOR OF THE LORD

What is the source of all this wealth? Did it come from the devil or from natural increase in the world? No, of course not. The Bible says that wealth comes from God.

Then Isaac sowed seed in that land and received in the same year a hundred times as much as he had planted, and the Lord favored him with blessings.

Genesis 26:12 AMP

It's obvious from this verse that Isaac's wealth came from God, because in the natural no farmer reaps a hundredfold harvest, particularly not in a year of drought. Why would God give him so much? Because abundance is His nature. He favored Isaac with enormous blessings.

However, God didn't bestow great blessings on Isaac just because He is a good God and loves to bless people. He favored

Isaac with great blessings because he was a sower and because he was the seed of Abraham.

And because New Testament believers are the seed of Abraham, we are in line to receive the blessings of the favor of God also.

JUST LIKE JOB

I heard someone say recently, "I am just like Job. It seems like everything goes wrong for me. I'll probably lose the house next." I wanted to say, "You probably will lose the house, talking like that." However, that is certainly not the way Job lived. Yes, he went through some horrible times, but these bad times only lasted nine months. After his bad times were over, God restored all he had lost and then some.

Therefore, if you are just like Job, you will be getting back at least twice as much as you lost. He got twice as many sheep, twice as many camels, twice as many donkeys, twice as many oxen. He had ten more children and lived to see his great-, great-grandchildren. He lived 140 more years! That doesn't sound too bad to me.

SOLOMON IN ALL HIS GLORY

If Abraham, Lot, Isaac and Job were billionaires, Solomon was a billionaire several times over. The Bible says he was richer than all who had gone before him.

So I was great, and increased more than all that were before me in Jerusalem: also my wisdom remained with me.

Ecclesiastes 2:9

As we've just seen, Solomon would have had to increase greatly to have been richer than anyone before him. His own father, David, was so wealthy that he gave more than a billion dollars in today's currency just in the building of the temple alone. And Solomon had more than that. In fact, the queen of Sheba, who was quite wealthy herself, was overwhelmed by Solomon's riches.

And when the queen of Sheba heard of the fame of Solomon concerning the name of the Lord, she came to prove him with hard questions. And she came to Jerusalem with a very great train, with camels that bare spices, and very much gold, and precious stones: and when she was come to Solomon, she communed with him of all that was in her heart. And Solomon told her all her questions: there was not any thing hid from the king, which he told her not. And when the queen of Sheba had seen all Solomon's wisdom, and the house that he had built, And the meat of his table, and the sitting of his servants, and the attendance of his ministers, and their apparel, and his cupbearers, and his ascent by which he went up unto the house of the Lord; there was no more spirit in her. And she said to the king, It was a true report that I heard in mine own land of thy acts and of thy wisdom. Howbeit I believed not the words, until I came, and mine eyes had seen it: and, behold, the half was not told me: thy wisdom and prosperity exceedeth the fame which I heard.

1 Kings 10:1-7

CONCLUSION

The men of God whom we looked at in this chapter— Abraham, Lot, Isaac, Job, David and Solomon—were all extremely wealthy, even by today's standards. However, as I said at the beginning of the chapter, we don't see that kind of wealth in the New Testament, because it had not been transferred into the Church yet. And before we see the promised wealth transfer come to pass, we have to be thoroughly familiar with, and able to practice, the scriptural principles I've been teaching in this book.

Let me review those principles for you briefly:

1. You have to know that prosperity is included in your redemption. You must understand that you have been redeemed from poverty by the blood of Jesus, as we studied in chapter 1.

2. You have to know the nature of God, that He's a good God and that He is a giver—not a taker. We studied God's nature in chapter 2.

3. You have to say the right thing. As we saw in chapter 3, confession is very important in obtaining the promises of God.

4. You have to sow seed properly. The process of sowing and reaping is God's method of blessing the Church. We studied the law of sowing and reaping in chapter 4.

5. You have to know what the Bible says about the wealth of the sinner that is laid up for you. The wealth of the sinner was covered in chapter 5.

6. You have to know what Jesus said about prosperity. We studied that in chapter 6.

7. You have to have New Testament Scriptures to back up anything you believe. And you need to know about the wealth in the Old Testament because it is in the process of being transferred to us. We covered that subject in this chapter.

8. Finally, you need to feed on prosperity Scriptures regularly. You should meditate on them, speak them and study them. The next chapter is designed for that purpose. There are many Scriptures that we have already used in this book, and I have added quite a few more. I also added other translations to help give a clear meaning of the verses. It is very important to renew your mind to God's Word.

God wants to make us rich, just as He made His people rich in the Old Testament. We have done the wrong things and said the wrong things for so long that it has been impossible for God to bless the body of Christ the way He has wanted to. Let's not hinder Him; let's cooperate with Him. Let's do everything we can to see His will fulfilled in the earth and to hasten the return of Jesus. He is only waiting for one thing—the precious fruit of the earth.

chapter eight

MEDITATION SCRIPTURES

INTRODUCTION

This chapter contains a tremendous key to walking in the abundance that God has provided for you. Whether you pick one Scripture a day or one Scripture a week, you should make meditation on the Word of God a regular part of your life.

To advance in your walk in the spirit, you must feed on the Word of God daily just as you feed your body natural food daily. You can't live spiritually on the Word you heard or read yesterday any more than you can live physically on the *memory* of the chicken salad you had for lunch yesterday. You must feed your natural body every day. And you must feed your spirit (the real you) at least as often.

To get the most spiritual nourishment from these Scriptures, go back and feast on them again and again. Meditate on them and confess them aloud until you know them by heart. Then begin applying them to your life. As I said at the beginning of this book, what you don't know can hurt you. Feed on the truth of God's Word, and the truth that you know will set you free to walk in God's abundance.

OLD TESTAMENT SCRIPTURES

And a river went out of Eden to water the garden; and from thence it was parted, and became into four heads. The name of the first is Pison: that is it which compasseth the whole land of Havilah, where there is gold; And the gold of that land is good....

Genesis 2:10-12

And I will make you a great nation, and I will bless you [with abundant increase of favors] and make your name famous and distinguished, and you will be a blessing [dispensing good to others].

Genesis 12:2 AMP

Now Abram was extremely rich in livestock and in silver and in gold.

Genesis 13:2 AMP

But Lot, who went with Abram, also had flocks and herds and tents. Now the land was not able to nourish and support them so they could dwell together, for their possessions were too great for them to live together.

Genesis 13:5,6 AMP

And the Lord hath blessed my master greatly; and he is become great: and he hath given him flocks, and herds, and silver, and gold, and menservants, and maidservants, and camels, and asses.

Genesis 24:35

Then Isaac sowed seed in that land and received in the same year a hundred times as much as he had planted, and the Lord favored him with blessings. And the man became great and gained more and more until he became very wealthy and distinguished; He owned flocks, herds, and a great supply of servants, and the Philistines envied him.

Genesis 26:12-14 AMP

And the man increased exceedingly, and had much cattle, and maidservants, and menservants, and camels, and asses. And he heard the words of Laban's sons, saying, Jacob hath taken away all that was our father's; and of that which was our father's hath he gotten all this glory.

Genesis 30:43;31:1

For their great flocks and herds and possessions [which they had collected] made it impossible for them to dwell together; the land in which they were strangers could not support them because of their livestock.

Genesis 36:7 AMP

But the Lord was with Joseph, and he [though a slave] was a successful and prosperous man; and he was in the house of his master the Egyptian. And [his master] saw that the Lord was with him and that the Lord made all that he did to flourish and succeed in his hand. So Joseph pleased [Potiphar] and found favor in his sight, and he served him. And [his master] made him supervisor over his house and he put all that he had in his charge.

Genesis 39:2-4 AMP

The prison warden paid no attention to anything that was in [Joseph's] charge, for the Lord was with him and made whatever he did to prosper.

Genesis 39:23 AMP

Little by little I will drive them out from before you, until you have increased and are numerous enough to take possession of the land.

Exodus 23:30 AMP

Take from among you an offering to the Lord. Whoever is of a willing and generous heart, let him bring the Lord's offering: gold, silver and bronze.

Exodus 35:5 AMP

And they came, each one whose heart stirred him up and whose spirit made him willing, and brought the Lord's offering to be used for the [new] Tent of Meeting, for all its service, and the holy garments.

Exodus 35:21 AMP

And they received of Moses all the offering, which the children of Israel had brought for the work of the service of the sanctuary, to make it withal. And they brought yet unto him free offerings every morning.

Exodus 36:3

And they spake unto Moses, saying, The people bring much more than enough for the service of the work, which the Lord commanded to make. And Moses gave commandment, and they caused it to be proclaimed throughout the camp, saying, Let neither man nor woman make any more work for the offering of the sanctuary. So the people were restrained from bringing. For the stuff they had was sufficient for all the work to make it, and too much.

Exodus 36:5-7

And you shall eat the [abundant] old store of produce long kept, and clear out the old [to make room] for the new.

Leviticus 26:10 AMP

And if you will go with us, it shall be that whatever good the Lord does to us, the same we will do to you.

Numbers 10:32 AMP

God is not a man, that he should lie; neither the son of man, that he should repent: hath he said, and shall he not do it? or hath he spoken, and shall he not make it good?

Numbers 23:19

Behold, the Lord thy God hath set the land before thee: go up and possess it, as the Lord God of thy fathers hath said unto thee; fear not, neither be discouraged.

Deuteronomy 1:21

And it shall be, when the Lord thy God shall have brought thee into the land which he sware unto thy fathers, to Abraham, to Isaac, and to Jacob, to give thee great and goodly cities, which thou buildedst not, And houses full of all good things, which thou filledst not, and wells digged, which thou diggedst not, vineyards and olive trees, which thou plantedst not; when thou shalt have eaten and be full.

Deuteronomy 6:10,11

But thou shalt remember the Lord thy God: for it is he that giveth thee power to get wealth, that he may establish his covenant which he sware unto thy fathers, as it is this day.

Deuteronomy 8:18

Always remember that it is the Lord your God who gives you power to become rich, and he does it to fulfill his promise to your ancestors.

Deuteronomy 8:18 TLB

And it shall come to pass, if thou shalt hearken diligently unto the voice of the Lord thy God, to observe and to do all his commandments which I command thee this day, that the Lord thy God will set thee on high above all nations of the earth: And all these blessings shall come on thee, and overtake thee, if thou shalt hearken unto the voice of the Lord thy God. Blessed shalt thou be in the city, and blessed shalt thou be in the field. Blessed shall be the fruit of thy body, and the fruit of thy ground, and the fruit of thy cattle, the increase of thy kine, and the flocks of thy sheep. Blessed shall be thy basket and thy store. Blessed shalt thou be when thou comest in, and blessed shalt thou be when thou goest out. The Lord shall cause thine enemies that rise up against thee to be smitten before thy face: they shall come out against thee one way, and flee before thee seven ways. The Lord shall command the blessing upon thee in thy storehouses, and in all that thou settest thine hand unto; and he shall bless thee in the land which the Lord thy God giveth thee. The Lord shall establish thee an holy people unto himself, as he hath sworn unto thee, if thou shalt keep the commandments of the Lord thy God, and walk in his ways. And all people of the earth shall see that thou art called by the name of the Lord; and they shall be afraid of thee. And the Lord shall make thee plenteous in goods, in the fruit of thy body, and in the fruit of thy cattle, and in the fruit of thy ground, in the land which the Lord sware unto thy fathers to give thee. The Lord shall open unto thee his good treasure, the heaven to give the rain unto thy land in his season, and to bless all the work of thine hand: and thou shalt lend unto many nations, and thou shalt not borrow. And the Lord shall make thee the head, and not the tail; and thou shalt be above only, and thou shalt not be beneath; if that thou hearken unto the commandments of the Lord thy God, which I command thee this day, to observe and to do them: And thou shalt not go aside from any of the words which I command thee this day, to the right hand, or to the left, to go after other gods to serve them.

Deuteronomy 28:1-14

And the Lord your God will make you abundantly prosperous in every work of your hand, in the fruit of your body, of your cattle, of your land, for good; for the Lord will again delight in prospering you, as He took delight in your fathers.

Deuteronomy 30:9 AMP

I call heaven and earth to record this day against you, that I have set before you life and death, blessing and cursing: therefore choose life, that both thou and thy seed may live.

Deuteronomy 30:19

Only be thou strong and very courageous, that thou mayest observe to do according to all the law, which Moses my servant commanded thee: turn not from it to the right hand or to the left, that thou mayest prosper whithersoever thou goest. This book of the law shall not depart out of thy mouth; but thou shalt meditate therein day and night, that thou mayest observe to do according to all that is written therein: for then thou shalt make thy way prosperous, and then thou shalt have good success.

Joshua 1:7,8

And Samuel grew, and the Lord was with him, and did let none of his words fall to the ground.

1 Samuel 3:19

And David recovered all that the Amalekites had carried away: and David rescued his two wives. And there was nothing lacking to them, neither small nor great, neither sons nor daughters, neither spoil, nor any thing that they had taken to them: David recovered all. And David took all the flocks and the herds, which they drave before those other cattle, and said, This is David's spoil.

1 Samuel 30:18-20

Blessed be the Lord, that hath given rest unto his people Israel, according to all that he promised: there hath not failed one word of all his good promise, which he promised by the hand of Moses his servant.

1 Kings 8:56

And when the queen of Sheba heard of the fame of Solomon concerning the name of the Lord, she came to prove him with hard questions. And she came to Jerusalem with a very great train, with camels that bare spices, and very much gold, and precious stones: and when she was come to Solomon, she communed with him of all that was in her heart. And Solomon told her all her questions: there was not any thing hid from the king, which he told her not. And when the queen of Sheba had seen all Solomon's wisdom, and the house that he had built, And the meat of his table, and the sitting of his servants, and the attendance of his ministers, and their apparel, and his cupbearers, and his ascent by which he went up unto the house of the Lord; there was no more spirit in her. And she said to the king, It was a true report that I heard in mine own land of thy acts and of thy wisdom. Howbeit I believed not the words, until I came, and mine eyes had seen it: and, behold, the half was not told me: thy wisdom and prosperity exceedeth the fame which I heard.

1 Kings 10:1-7

And she went and did according to the saying of Elijah: and she, and he, and her house did eat many days.

1 Kings 17:15

Wisdom and knowledge is granted unto thee; and I will give thee riches, and wealth, and honour, such as none of the kings have had that have been before thee, neither shall there any after thee have the like.

2 Chronicles 1:12

When Jehoshaphat and his people came to take the spoil, they found among them much cattle, goods, garments, and precious things which they took for themselves, more than they could carry away, so much they were three days in gathering the spoil.

2 Chronicles 20:25 AMP

Then answered I them, and said unto them, The God of heaven, he will prosper us....

Nehemiah 2:20

This is the portion of a wicked man with God, and the heritage of oppressors, which they shall receive of the Almighty....

Though he heap up silver as the dust, and prepare raiment as the clay; He may prepare it, but the just shall put it on, and the innocent shall divide the silver.

Job 27:13,16,17

If they obey and serve him, they shall spend their days in prosperity, and their years in pleasures.

Job 36:11

Blessed is the man that walketh not in the counsel of the ungodly, nor standeth in the way of sinners, nor sitteth in the seat of the scornful. But his delight is in the law of the Lord; and in his law doth he meditate day and night. And he shall be like a tree planted by the rivers of water, that bringeth forth his fruit in his season; his leaf also shall not wither; and whatsoever he doeth shall prosper.

Psalm 1:1-3

The Lord is my shepherd; I shall not want.

Psalm 23:1

The Eternal shepherds me, I lack for nothing.

Psalm 23:1 Moffatt

Jehovah is my shepherd, I do not lack.

Psalm 23:1 Young[1]

The Lord is my shepherd; how can I lack anything?

Psalm 23:1 Knox[2]

The earth is the Lord's, and the fulness thereof; the world, and they that dwell therein.

Psalm 24:1

O fear the Lord, ye his saints: for there is no want to them that fear him. The young lions do lack, and suffer hunger: but they that seek the Lord shall not want any good thing.

Psalm 34:9,10

If you belong to the Lord, reverence him; for everyone who does this has everything he needs. Even strong young lions sometimes go hungry, but those of us who reverence the Lord will never lack any good thing.

Psalm 34:9,10 TLB

Let them shout for joy, and be glad, that favour my righteous cause: yea, let them say continually, Let the Lord be magnified, which hath pleasure in the prosperity of his servant.

Psalm 35:27

"...All hail to the Eternal, who loves to see his servant prospering!"

Psalm 35:27 Moffatt

Trust in the Lord, and do good; so shalt thou dwell in the land, and verily thou shalt be fed. Delight thyself also in the Lord; and he shall give thee the desires of thine heart. Commit thy way unto the Lord; trust also in him; and he shall bring it to pass.

Psalm 37:3-5

For every beast of the forest is mine, and the cattle upon a thousand hills.

Psalm 50:10

Thou hast caused men to ride over our heads; we went through fire and through water: but thou broughtest us out into a wealthy place.

Psalm 66:12

Then shall the earth yield her increase; and God, even our own God, shall bless us.

Psalm 67:6

Blessed be the Lord, who daily loadeth us with benefits, even the God of our salvation. Selah.

Psalm 68:19

[He] brought his people safely out from Egypt, loaded with silver and gold; there were no sick and feeble folk among them then.

Psalm 105:37 TLB

And gave them the lands of the nations [of Canaan], and they reaped the fruits of those peoples' labor.

Psalm 105:44 AMP

Wealth and riches shall be in his house: and his righteousness endureth for ever.

Psalm 112:3

Ease shall dwell in his house, and great prosperity...

Psalm 112:3 Knox[3]

He raiseth up the poor out of the dust, and lifteth the needy out of the dunghill; That he may set him with princes, even with the princes of his people.

Psalm 113:7,8

The Lord shall increase you more and more; you and your children.

Psalm 115:14

Save now, I beseech thee, O Lord: O Lord, I beseech thee, send now prosperity.

Psalm 118:25

For ever, O Lord, thy word is settled in heaven.

Psalm 119:89

Honour the Lord with thy substance, and with the firstfruits of all thine increase: So shall thy barns be filled with plenty, and thy presses shall burst out with new wine.

Proverbs 3:9,10

I wisdom dwell with prudence, and find out knowledge of witty inventions.

Proverbs 8:12

That I may cause those that love me to inherit substance; and I will fill their treasures.

Proverbs 8:21

Those who love and follow me are indeed wealthy. I fill their treasuries.

Proverbs 8:21 TLB

The blessing of the Lord, it maketh rich, and he addeth no sorrow with it.

Proverbs 10:22

Of the Lord's gift comes wealth without drudgery.

Proverbs 10:22 Knox[4]

There is that scattereth, and yet increaseth; and there is that withholdeth more than is meet, but it tendeth to poverty.

Proverbs 11:24

A good man leaveth an inheritance to his children's children: and the wealth of the sinner is laid up for the just.

Proverbs 13:22

A man's gift maketh room for him, and bringeth him before great men.

Proverbs 18:16

He that hath pity upon the poor lendeth unto the Lord; and that which he hath given will he pay him again.

Proverbs 19:17

When you're kind to the poor, you lend to the Lord, and he'll pay you back for what you do.

Proverbs 19:17 Beck

The rich ruleth over the poor, and the borrower is servant to the lender.

Proverbs 22:7

He who by charging excessive interest and who by unjust efforts to get gain increases his material possession gathers it for him [to spend] who is kind and generous to the poor.

Proverbs 28:8 AMP

He that giveth unto the poor shall not lack: but he that hideth his eyes shall have many a curse.

Proverbs 28:27

For God giveth to a man that is good in his sight wisdom, and knowledge, and joy: but to the sinner he giveth travail, to gather and to heap up, that he may give to him that is good before God....

Ecclesiastes 2:26

Give generously, for your gifts will return to you later. Divide your gifts among many, for in the days ahead you yourself may need much help.

Ecclesiastes 11:1,2 TLB

If ye be willing and obedient, ye shall eat the good of the land.

Isaiah 1:19

If you will only let me help you, if you will only obey, then I will make you rich!

Isaiah 1:19 TLB

And ye shall eat plenty, and be satisfied, and praise the name of the Lord your God, that hath dealt wondrously with you: and my people shall never be ashamed.

Joel 2:26

...I will fill this house with glory, saith the Lord of hosts. The silver is mine, and the gold is mine, saith the Lord of hosts. The glory of this latter house shall be greater than of the former....

Haggai 2:7-9

Will a man rob God? Yet ye have robbed me. But ye say, Wherein have we robbed thee? In tithes and offerings. Ye are cursed with a curse: for ye have robbed me, even this whole nation. Bring ye all the tithes into the storehouse, that there may be meat in mine house, and prove me now herewith, saith the Lord of hosts, if I will not open you the windows of heaven, and pour you out a blessing, that there shall not be room enough to receive it. And I will rebuke the devourer for your sakes, and he shall not destroy the fruits of your ground; neither shall your vine cast her fruit before the time in the field, saith the Lord of hosts.

Malachi 3:8-11

NEW TESTAMENT SCRIPTURES

Lay not up for yourselves treasures upon earth, where moth and rust doth corrupt, and where thieves break through and steal: But lay up for yourselves treasures in heaven, where neither moth nor rust doth corrupt, and where thieves do not break through nor steal: For where your treasure is, there will your heart be also.

Matthew 6:19-21

But seek ye first the kingdom of God, and his righteousness; and all these things shall be added unto you.

Matthew 6:33

If ye then, being evil, know how to give good gifts unto your children, how much more shall your Father which is in heaven give good things to them that ask him?

Matthew 7:11

And if you hardhearted, sinful men know how to give good gifts to your children, won't your father in heaven even more certainly give good gifts to those who ask him for them?

Matthew 7:11 TLB

If you, then, being human respond to the legitimate desires and needs of your children, do you not know that to a greater extent, your Father, the source of all being, will give you the true needs and desires of your life?

Matthew 7:11 Johnson[5]

Notwithstanding, lest we should offend them, go thou to the sea, and cast an hook, and take up the fish that first cometh up; and when thou hast opened his mouth, thou shalt find a piece of money: that take, and give unto them for me and thee.

Matthew 17:27

And these are they which are sown on good ground; such as hear the word, and receive it, and bring forth fruit, some thirtyfold, some sixty, and some an hundred.

Mark 4:20

If any man have ears to hear, let him hear. And he said unto them, Take heed what ye hear: with what measure ye mete, it shall be measured to you: and unto you that hear shall more be given.

Mark 4:23,24

And he said, So is the kingdom of God, as if a man should cast seed into the ground.

Mark 4:26

And Jesus answered and said, Verily I say unto you, There is no man that hath left house, or brethren, or sisters, or father, or mother, or wife, or children, or lands, for my sake, and the gospel's, But he shall receive an hundredfold now in this time, houses, and brethren, and sisters, and mothers, and children, and lands, with persecutions; and in the world to come eternal life.

Mark 10:29,30

And Jesus sat over against the treasury, and beheld how the people cast money into the treasury: and many that were rich cast in much. And there came a certain poor widow, and she threw in two mites, which make a farthing. And he called unto him his disciples, and saith unto them, Verily I say unto you, That this poor widow hath cast more in, than all they which have cast into the treasury: For all they did cast in of their abundance; but she of her want did cast in all that she had, even all her living.

Mark 12:41-44

For with God nothing is ever impossible and no word from God shall be without power or impossible of fulfillment.

Luke 1:37 AMP

Now when he had left speaking, he said unto Simon, Launch out into the deep, and let down your nets for a draught. And Simon answering said unto him, Master, we have toiled all the night, and have taken nothing: nevertheless at thy word I will let down the net. And when they had this done, they inclosed a great multitude of fishes: and their net brake. And they beckoned unto their partners, which were in the other ship, that they should come and help them. And they came, and filled both the ships, so that they began to sink.

Luke 5:4-7

Give, and it shall be given unto you; good measure, pressed down, and shaken together, and running over, shall men give into your bosom. For with the same measure that ye mete withal it shall be measured to you again.

Luke 6:38

For if you give, you will get! Your gift will return to you in full and overflowing measure, pressed down, shaken together to make room for more, and running over. Whatever measure you use to give—large or small—will be used to measure what is given back to you.

Luke 6:38 TLB

And Joanna the wife of Chuza Herod's steward, and Susanna, and many others, which ministered unto him of their substance.

Luke 8:3

And he said unto him, Son, thou art ever with me, and all that I have is thine.

Luke 15:31

I sent you to reap that whereon ye bestowed no labour: other men laboured, and ye are entered into their labours.

John 4:38

There was a certain man in Caesarea called Cornelius, a centurion of the band called the Italian band, A devout man, and one that feared God with all his house, which gave much alms to the people, and prayed to God alway. He saw in a vision evidently about the ninth hour of the day an angel of God coming in to him, and saying unto him, Cornelius. And when he looked on him, he was afraid, and said, What is it, Lord? And he said unto him, Thy prayers and thine alms are come up for a memorial before God.

Acts 10:1-4

He that spared not his own Son, but delivered him up for us all, how shall he not with him also freely give us all things?

Romans 8:32

If God did not spare his only son, but gave him up for the sake of us all, can we not be sure that with him there is nothing that he will not freely give us?

Romans 8:32 Barclay

He did not spare his own Son, but gave him up for us all; and with this gift how can he fail to lavish upon us all he has to give?

Romans 8:32 NEB

I have planted, Apollos watered; but God gave the increase. So then neither is he that planteth any thing, neither he that watereth; but God that giveth the increase.

1 Corinthians 3:6,7

Even so hath the Lord ordained that they which preach the gospel should live of the gospel.

1 Corinthians 9:14

For the earth is the Lord's, and the fulness thereof.

1 Corinthians 10:26

For ye know the grace of our Lord Jesus Christ, that, though he was rich, yet for your sakes he became poor, that ye through his poverty might be rich.

2 Corinthians 8:9

[Remember] this: he who sows sparingly and grudgingly will also reap sparingly and grudgingly, and he who sows generously [that blessings may come to someone] will also reap generously and with blessings. Let each one [give] as he had made up his own mind and purposed in his heart, not reluctantly or sorrowfully or under compulsion, for God loves (He takes pleasure in, prizes above other things, and is unwilling to abandon or do without) a cheerful (joyous, "prompt to do it") giver [whose heart is in his giving]. And God is able to make all grace (every favor and earthly blessing) come to you in abundance, so that you may always and under all circumstances and whatever the need be self-sufficient [possessing enough to require no aid or support and furnished in abundance for every good work and charitable donation].

2 Corinthians 9:6-8 AMP

Now he that ministereth seed to the sower both minister bread for your food, and multiply your seed sown, and increase the fruits of your righteousness.

2 Corinthians 9:10

Christ hath redeemed us from the curse of the law, being made a curse for us: for it is written, Cursed is every one that hangeth on a tree: That the blessing of Abraham might come on the Gentiles through Jesus Christ; that we might receive the promise of the Spirit through faith.

Galatians 3:13,14

But Christ has bought us out from under the doom of that impossible system by taking the curse for our wrongdoing upon himself. For it is written in the Scripture, "Anyone who is hanged on a tree is cursed" [as Jesus was hung upon a wooden cross]. Now God can bless the Gentiles, too, with this same blessing he promised to Abraham; and all of us as Christians can have the promised Holy Spirit through this faith.

Galatians 3:13,14 TLB

And if ye be Christ's, then are ye Abraham's seed, and heirs according to the promise.

Galatians 3:29

Let him who receives instruction in the Word [of God] share all good things with his teacher [contributing to his support].

Galatians 6:6 AMP

Be not deceived; God is not mocked: for whatsoever a man soweth, that shall he also reap.

Galatians 6:7

Now unto him that is able to do exceeding abundantly above all that we ask or think, according to the power that worketh in us.

Ephesians 3:20

Let him that stole steal no more: but rather let him labour, working with his hands the thing which is good, that he may have to give to him that needeth.

Ephesians 4:28

Knowing that whatsoever good thing any man doeth, the same shall he receive of the Lord....

Ephesians 6:8

But my God shall supply all your need according to his riches in glory by Christ Jesus.

Philippians 4:19

For the love of money is the root of all evil: which while some coveted after, they have erred from the faith, and pierced themselves through with many sorrows.

1 Timothy 6:10

Charge them that are rich in this world, that they be not highminded, nor trust in uncertain riches, but in the living God, who giveth us richly all things to enjoy.

1 Timothy 6:17

Beloved, I wish above all things that thou mayest prosper and be in health, even as thy soul prospereth.

3 John 2

Beloved, I pray that you may prosper in all things and be in health, just as your soul prospers.

3 John 2 NKJV

For these [traveling missionaries] have gone out for the Name's sake (for His sake) and are accepting nothing from the Gentiles (the heathen, the non-Israelites). So we ourselves ought to support such people [to welcome and provide for them], in order that we may be fellow workers in the Truth (the whole Gospel) and cooperate with its teachers.

3 John 7,8 AMP

ENDNOTES

Chapter 1

[1] The term "spiritual death" is used in this instance to differentiate for the reader the various aspects of redemption secured for us by Jesus on the cross. I am referring to redemption from spiritual death here primarily as salvation from hell and entrance into heaven upon a person's physical death. However, I wish to clarify that scripturally, spiritual death involves much more than a sinner's ultimate condemnation to hell. Being redeemed from spiritual death also means to be alive spiritually while walking on the earth, to be renewed continually in one's inner man. For clarity, however, I am referring in this book to the ultimate aspect of our redemption from spiritual death, salvation from hell.

[2] Strong, James. "Greek Dictionary of the New Testament," *Strong's Exhaustive Concordance of the Bible,* (Nashville: Abingdon, 1890), 34, #2172

[3] I am using the phrase *spiritual prosperity* here to mean "nonmaterial or inner prosperity" as opposed to material or outer prosperity, that is, physical and financial prosperity. As I am using it in this book, *spiritual prosperity* is everything that has to do with the inner man, including both *soul* (Strong's #5590) and *spirit* (Strong's #4151). For a discussion of the distinction between man's soul and his spirit, see Kenneth Hagin's book *How You Can Be Led by the Spirit of God,* (Tulsa, Oklahoma: Kenneth Hagin Ministries, 1989), 9-15.

Chapter 8

[1] Young, Robert. *Young's Literal Translation of the Holy Bible.* Rev. ed. (Grand Rapids, MI: Baker Book House, 1953), 360.

[2] Knox. *The Holy Bible. A Translation From the Latin Vulgate in the Light of the Hebrew and Greek Originals.* (New York: Sheed & Ward, Inc., 1944, 1948, 1950), 487.

[3] Ibid., 525.

[4] Ibid., 545.

[5] Johnson, Ben Campbell. *Matthew and Mark. A Relational Paraphrase.* (Waco, TX: Word, Inc., 1978), 29.

ABOUT THE AUTHOR

RayGene Wilson is an anointed minister who is recognized as one who will boldly preach and sing the uncompromised Word of God. He has been in full-time ministry since 1979 and is an ordained minister with Kenneth Copeland Ministries. He has ministered with various music ministries over the years and has appeared on every major Christian television program in America. RayGene traveled full-time with Kenneth Hagin for several years and has ministered in Kenneth Copeland's Believers' Conventions worldwide. He has recorded many albums, including four solo albums to date, and he is the author of the book *In Spirit and in Truth: The Power of New Testament Praise and Worship.*

In 1991 he married Beth Hogue from Nashville, Tennessee. Beth is also an ordained minister and is a graduate of The University of Mississippi, Rhema Bible Training Center and Victory Bible Training Center in Nashville. Together they travel around the world, taking God's Word and the move of the Holy Ghost to the nations.

To contact RayGene Wilson,

write:

RayGene Wilson Ministries

P.O. Box 4779

Tulsa, Oklahoma 74159

www.raygene.com

Please include your prayer requests and comments

when you write.

OTHER BOOKS BY RAYGENE WILSON

*In Spirit and in Truth: The Power of New Testament
Praise and Worship*

Available from your local bookstore.

HARRISON HOUSE
Tulsa, Oklahoma 74153

THE HARRISON HOUSE VISION

Proclaiming the truth and the power
Of the Gospel of Jesus Christ
With excellence;

Challenging Christians to
Live victoriously,
Grow spiritually,
Know God intimately.